Dancing Between Two Worlds
Jung and the Native American Soul

Other Books in the Jung and Spirituality Series

CARL JUNG AND CHRISTIAN SPIRITUALITY
Edited by Robert L. Moore

JUNG AND CHRISTIANITY IN DIALOGUE
Faith, Feminism, and Hermeneutics
Edited by Robert L. Moore
and Daniel J. Meckel

LORD OF THE FOUR QUARTERS
The Mythology of Kingship
by John Weir Perry

THE WEB OF THE UNIVERSE
Jung, the "New Physics," and Human Spirituality
by John Hitchcock

SELF AND LIBERATION
The Jung-Buddhism Dialogue
Edited by Daniel J. Meckel
and Robert L. Moore

THE UNCONSCIOUS CHRISTIAN
Images of God in Dreams
by James A. Hall
Edited by Daniel J. Meckel

INDIVIDUATION AND THE ABSOLUTE
Hegel, Jung, and the Path Toward Wholeness
by Sean M. Kelly

JESUS' PARABLES
Finding Our God Within
by Robert Winterhalter with George W. Fisk

IN GOD'S SHADOW
The Collaboration of Victor White
and C.G. Jung
by Ann Conrad Lammers

Dancing Between Two Worlds

JUNG AND THE NATIVE AMERICAN SOUL

Fred R. Gustafson

Paulist Press
New York ✧ Mahwah, N.J.

Cover art courtesy of Claudia DeLong Pope, Silverton, Colorado.

Cover design by Kathy McKeen.

Library of Congress Cataloging-in-Publication Data

Gustafson, Fred.
Dancing between two worlds : Jung and the Native American soul / Fred R. Gustafson.
p. cm.–(Jung and spirituality series)
Includes bibliographical references and index.
ISBN 0-8091-3693-7
1. Indians of North America–Religion. 2. Indian philosophy–North America. 3. Psychoanalysis and religion–North America. 4. Spiritual healing–North America. 5. Jung, C.G. (Carl Gustav), 1875-1961. I. Title. II. Series: Jung and spirituality.
E98.R3G97 1996
299′.7–dc20 96-41257
CIP

Published by Paulist Press
997 Macarthur Boulevard
Mahwah, New Jersey 07430

Printed and bound in the
United States of America

Contents

SERIES FOREWORD

The Jung and Spirituality series provides a forum for the critical interaction between Jungian psychology and living spiritual traditions. The series serves two important goals.

The first goal is: *To enhance a creative exploration of the contributions and criticisms that Jung's psychology can offer to religion.* Jungian thought has far-reaching implications for the understanding and practice of spirituality. Interest in these implications continues to expand in both Christian and non-Christian religious communities. People are increasingly aware of the depth and insight that a Jungian perspective adds to the human experiences of the sacred. And yet, the use of Jungian psychoanalysis clearly does not eliminate the need for careful philosophical, theological and ethical reflection or for maintaining one's centeredness in a spiritual tradition.

The second goal is: *To bring the creative insights and critical tools of religious studies and practice to bear on Jungian thought.* Many volumes in the Jung and Spirituality series work to define the borders of the Jungian and spiritual traditions, to bring the spiritual dimensions of Jung's work into relief, and to deepen those dimensions. We believe that an important outcome of the Jung-Spirituality dialogue is greater cooperation of psychology and spirituality. Such cooperation will move us ahead in the formation of a post-modern spirituality, equal to the challenges of the twenty-first century.

Robert L. Moore
Series Editor

Preface

Every couple of weeks I take some time to browse through some of our local bookstores. I am amazed at the variety of new volumes that are offered on so many subjects. The reading public seems to yearn for information and affirmation concerning how to live with more meaning. It used to be that we would get information about how to fix up our houses, cars, and our yards, and about how to take care of our children and our relationships. Today we are seeking ways that will feed our souls. In a mainstream world of hustle and bustle, fluster and flurry, bulging planner books, chaos, and violence of every kind, our bodies and souls need a more conscientious effort to maintain balance and simplicity in our lives. As an urbanite and a pastor of an inner city congregation, I see the intense and immediate need to reconnect with the best of ourselves, our family and friends, and our community. I am pleased that *Dancing Between Two Worlds* reminds us of the importance of seeking out the basic gifts given to each and every one of us, the gift of life on this earth, our relationship to one another and to all of creation, and living life to the fullest.

In the busy world of urban life—where most things that happen are ruled by the clock, which seems to run faster and faster every year—I crave those special moments that help me to reconnect with activity that grounds me, strengthens me, and uplifts me. Such was the occasion recently. I was visiting Lakota friends on their reservation. It was a perfect evening: a moonlit night, cool breezes after a hot day, and friends visiting with each other. There was a camp fire, lots of good stories, and laughter illuminating the prairie night. People were snacking on leftovers, fruit, and assorted sweets. We were camped near sacred ceremonial grounds. One of the women suggested that at midnight we should have a women's *inipi* (a sweat lodge). Four of us agreed and walked over to the ceremonial fire where we could heat up seven large rocks. We sat on the ground and visited while waiting for the rocks to get hot. The flames leaped and danced in rhythm to the gentle breezes that flowed over the rocks, heating them gently. The evening breeze danced on to touch the rest of the sleepy camps. It was truly a beautiful night. Once the rocks were ready, they were placed in a small pit in the center of the small lodge where the four women were seated in a circle on the cool earth. Water was brought in and special songs were sung in thanksgiving for the fire, water, and rocks that were helping us during this special prayer time. Simple voices raised up powerful songs of thanksgiving. It didn't matter how good any of our voices were, nor did it matter if one of us made a mistake in not knowing all the words or the tune. We gave our best. There was no judgment. During our prayers, water was poured on the hot rocks, opening up the pores of our skin in order to cleanse us. All the residues of dust and dirt were carried away in small streams of water dripping into the earth.

The prayers from the deepest part of our hearts were for ourselves, our families, and our communities, asking that we do better in taking care of one another, petitioning for help and healing, and offering thanksgiving for all people and situations we could think of. There was no watch, nor was anyone concerned about how long this ceremony was taking. It took as long as it needed. Our bodies were sweating from the heat of the rocks and the moisture in the lodge. Burdens were lifted from our heavy hearts. We began to feel good in what otherwise could be an uncomfortable situation. We were being cleansed inside and out, releasing our anguishes and asking for help for ourselves and our communities. As we sat on the earth in this humble dwelling with steam rising from hot rocks and prayers from our darkest places, our hearts, minds, and bodies were purified. Songs of thanksgiving were sung and the door was opened, spilling steam into the refreshing breezes of the night. A cup of water was given to each woman to drink.

This special gathering was simple, good, and vital. It met some basic needs: literally touching the earth and using basic elements (fire, water, rock, steam) of the earth to assist us in our ceremony of prayer, being together in community and sharing needs, and helping one another. These four women may never meet together again, but for this particular event, they journeyed together with a chance to nourish and feed their souls, spirits, and bodies.

Not everyone will have a chance to make this particular journey that I shared, but my brother Fred urges each one of us in the following chapters of *Dancing Between Two Worlds* to seek our own indigenous roots, which are grounded in "an attitude and a way of life that respects the unity and relationship of all things on the earth." Through his own journey of life-giving experiences with other groups of people, his dreams, and his educational endeavors, he becomes a gentle town crier reminding us of what to take with us as we move through our own journey on this earth.

I'm glad that he chose to share some of his experiences in Indian country, especially the understanding he was taught through the Lakota prayer, "*Mitakuye Oyasin.*" This prayer for all creation and the created order is more vital now than ever in a world that is suffering from so much disconnection, chaos, and violence. At times, we seem to be holding on to a tiny thread of goodwill toward one another instead of relishing in good relationships. Many of our sacred places are now surrounded by polluted water and air and other poisons. This prayer is for all of us, for we are relatives to each other. As relatives let us pray for harmony among all of the people, the earth, and all that is. As we begin a new century, let us bring forth the best of all we have been given and join in the dance of the Universe, seeking love and peace, joy and happiness, for its inhabitants.

Marlene Whiterabbit Helgemo
Minneapolis
1996

Foreword

Fred Gustafson's book, *Dancing Between Two Worlds,* is written not only for Jungian psychologists but also for lay people, Native Americans, environmentalists and all people indigenous to the earth itself who suffer concern for its future. It is an account no one of us should overlook because it not only states the present psychological and spiritual dilemma but also gives solutions.

Gustafson's style is deeply warm and appreciative of the plight of the Native American on our continent. He consistently reminds the reader how the mutual tragic five hundred year history of two cultures has done spiritual damage to both. At the same time, he also envisions how the Indian holds the key to the secrets of nature through a spiritual attitude and understanding that holds all life as sacred no matter how insignificant it may appear. All of life stands in a living relationship to everything else, including human beings. He states that this incarnational view has been sorely lacking in our dominant European culture. To understand this is essential in making a lasting stand for nature's preservation–the one and only hope for planet Earth.

The Contents gives an indication of the wealth of feeling that flows out of this author who has taken the problems we now face as personal to himself. Chapter Three, "The Collective Search: An American Metaphor, "Dances with Wolves," is especially moving. I had seen the videotape and already felt its powerful message and knew of its unusual popularity. Gustafson interprets it into our western Anglo language in a way that elucidates the cultural issues facing us all. In his treatment of the story, he opens a vista into C.G. Jung's psychological discoveries and experiences of the deep levels of the unconscious. He shows how this film touches on the archetypal depths of the psyche that, when fully experienced, bring about changes of attitude. I think of them as inner psychic levels that correspond outwardly to what we know as wilderness and whatever truly natural areas are still left. Native Americans already had long ago inherited from their ancestors a conversant relation to these inner and outer psychic wilderness levels. This heritage accounts for their powerful emotional defense of the land that they know as Mother and Grandmother.

Gustafson's book is real and far from being sentimental. When he relates the Indian view of matter as being alive, he refers to the modern physicist's view that matter is made up of atoms that are ever in motion. Matter, indeed, is a living Mother to us all.

I feel validated in my own empathy with the Native American from reading this manuscript. It reassures me more than any writing I have so far encountered. My own European ancestors set foot on Connecticut soil in the early 1600s. My grandfather drove sheep across the continent from Ohio to feed the miners in California during the mid-1800s. We planted our roots in one of the world's most beautiful coastlines where we would mingle with the Chumash both materially and spiritually. My grandfather had no trouble with the Indian people en route to this land because, as he said, "If you are courteous with them, they do not bother you." He may have had something to do with my own liking of Native Americans. The generation after him subscribed to the idea: "The only good Indian is a dead Indian." Fortunately, I shut my ears to such pronouncements. I was raised from infancy on this coastal southern California tract of land that would become a wild cattle ranch. The area had been untouched by any white people. It once was the background of many Chumash villages and especially Chumash fishermen. As children, my twin brother and I would explore the area, finding Chumash artifacts, even some Chumash skeletal remains, but no one told us about the people themselves. When I became a teenager, I joined in with the vaqueros on cattle roundups. Some of these men were descendants of the few remaining Chumash in southern California. They were skillful horsemen and were in demand by the local ranchers. They taught me all I know about cattle ranching–not to mention the fact that they were very good to me. I got my start in appreciating these indigenous humans in our own back yard. From that point on, I had to read the anthropologists for any further understanding. My liking of these people was all that supported me until much later when books written by Native Americans themselves helped me to recognize through them my own natural affinity for nature.

And here is the key point of Gustafson's book. Having read it twice, I can understand how my own love of the land and my feeling for the original peoples of this land are also reflective of my own indigenous soul. Anyone who loses this connection or projects it on another not only grieves but suffers a loss of soul. I am one of the "indigenous ones" Gustafson speaks of and challenges us all to reclaim.

In closing, I recommend Chapter Four, "A Personal Search: Seeking the Ancestor." Here it is most evident that Gustafson took the time to reach into the Native American heart and mind, allowing himself to be not only influenced but also changed by this encounter. This is reflected in how his own unconscious responded. Here, with his extraordinary generosity, Gustafson has given us many of his own dreams as examples of deep archetypal manifestations of the psyche, making collective parallels that reinforce the content of this remarkable book.

Jane Hollister Wheelwright, A.L.A.
Jungian Analyst
May 1995

To quote my friend, Erik Erikson, "I could not disagree less" with Jane's summary of this book by Fred Gustafson. Speaking for myself, three foci stand out. First, this valuable book opens the doors to the archetypal world and the Self of which Jung speaks. Secondly, Gustafson's acceptance of the Lakota Sioux and their acceptance of him stand out as a specific recognition that the Universe sees all peoples as one. This oneness knows that no human being or group runs life or the Universe but is simply a part of it. Thirdly, he shows that the path of wisdom and salvation cannot be discovered from the outside-inward. The only solution comes from the inside-outward, a point Jung continually made.

Joseph B. Wheelwright, M.D.
Jungian Analyst
May 1996

Introduction

Just what this book is about can partly be expressed in a short vignette. It is a personal story based on an irrational fear that would not leave me, one of those fears most people keep to themselves. It was specific to a portion of land shared in common with some friends, land I am familiar with, deeply love and am committed to. Simply stated, my fear had to do with walking this land at nighttime. This was not a fear of people but simply a fear of the darkness of the wooded area itself. There were trails throughout this property that I was very familiar with and had walked over many times. To add to the irrationality, it should be mentioned that I am not afraid of wooded areas or wilderness adventures, yet, for some reason, walking these trails at nighttime unnerved me.

About three years prior to this writing, I said to myself, "Enough of this. I am going to take a night walk. I am going to face up to this fear once and for all, instead of avoiding it, and see where it takes me." And that I did. I clearly remember entering the heavily wooded area that night. It was a moonless evening, quite dark, and once on the inner wooded trail, it was black, even blacker than black. The path that was so familiar in the daylight hours was now only a guess. Proceeding with care and some uncertainty I headed in a direction that would take me into a clearing that I knew would give me some orientation. When I did, I saw what I had seen many times before in my life, but now, with the wooded path behind me, it seemed like the first time ever. Here were stars unnumbered; here too were constellations in all their clarity; there across the night sky was the path of our own galaxy, provoking the imagination of countless galaxies beyond our own and of a limitless universe. Here were wonder, awe, and respect that required the only proper response–silence.

I no longer have the irrational fear of walking at nighttime in the wooded area. If I ever would, it would be for well-grounded reasons. What was once irrationality is now a longing for such an experience, a longing that is fulfilled on most occasions. What happened to me that night was not a moving beyond my own inner darkness but rather some reconciliation with it as the custodian of that ancient, equally dark primordial history we all carry. However, the blessing came in knowing more than ever that this too is part of a greater cosmic story of which we are all a part. The irrationality of my original fear could not survive this truth.

This book deals with fear and longing but of a specific kind. It is a response to a fear of the earth itself that is manifested in so many ways in so many places in our times and that has produced so much human anguish. It is designed for the western mind-set that sees the earth, one's own earthly body and anything representing the earth as a dark trail best left to be avoided. This fear has produced an alienation of modern humankind from one another and set the stage for personal and collective projections on anyone who can carry what we fear. The alienation is also toward our own ancestral past, that dark evolutionary night from which we all came, that mothered us into our present form. Throughout these chapters, I refer to the "Indigenous One" as a reference point for the antiquity of the human soul. We came from somewhere. We have emerged with the rest of creation along an evolutionary path that is integral to the earth itself. For some reason there is a fear of these roots and of making our connection with the whole of creation. Our own inner Indigenous Ancestor has been pushed aside and all but forgotten. If the entire book can be put into one thought it is this: not only have we lost a connection to our own indigenous root, but alongside this there exists a profound sadness and longing for its return. This whole idea came to me in the fall of 1990 through a dream anticipating the forthcoming recognition of the centennial of the Massacre of Wounded Knee, December 29, 1890. This dream was the main impetus for writing this book, the reasons for which I more clearly describe in Chapter One. It is enough to state here that I know now that the collective issue cannot stay at the level of guilt and blame for all the violations done but must be understood as a common collective grief shared by all. The bottom line is that we are all humans, children of the earth, whether we know it or not and thus share Her antiquity.

In 1931 Dr. Carl Jung wrote in "Archaic Man:"[1] "...it is not only primitive man whose psychology is archaic. It is the psychology also of modern civilized man....On the contrary, every civilized human being, however high his conscious development, is still an archaic man at the deeper levels of his psyche." That we have now all but forgotten this has produced the modern malady of soul known as alienation. This is an alienation from our deeper self, from the earth as home and from the gained wisdom of our evolutionary past. It has set us adrift to project these losses on identified indigenous peoples of the world with the result of either idealizing or romanticizing them according to our undifferentiated needs or conquering and attempting to destroy them to rid the truth they carry from our terrified and, as I stated, alienated ego. If this were only on a personal level, it would be bad enough. However, it has been raised to collective proportions, institutionalized, politicized and made a way of life in the world affected by the western perspective of life. But what is this perspective? Jung, in the same writing, clearly states that one of the dominant tenets in our western world is the profound belief in the supremacy of causality. He states: "It is a rational presupposition of ours that everything has a natural and perceptible cause. We are convinced of this right from the start. Causality is one of our most sacred dogmas....We distinctly resent the idea of invisible and arbitrary forces, for it is not so long ago that we made our escape from that frightening world of dreams and superstitions, and constructed for ourselves a picture of the cosmos worthy of our rational consciousness–that latest and greatest achievement of man. We are now surrounded by a world that is obedient to rational laws....Chance happenings are repellent to the mind that loves order. They disturb the regular, predictable course of events in the most absurd and irritating way. We resent them as much as we resent invisible, arbitrary forces....They are the worst enemies of our careful calculations and a continual threat to all our undertakings. Being admittedly contrary to reason, they deserve all our abuse...."[2]

Everywhere this has affected how we do business in the western world, whether in our politics, our vocations, our educational system or our religious beliefs which are of Judeo-Christian origin. The historical problem is exposed when Jung dismantles this worldview: "If we consider the matter, we could as well say that the causal connection of events according to general laws is a theory which is borne out about half the time, while for the rest the demon of chance holds sway."[3] But "chance" is a pejorative term. What Jung defends in the primitive regions of our soul is the place of "intention" which opens the mind to forces beyond the ego, to angels, archangels, principalities, spirits and the reality of archetypes and the central organizing principle of the Self. "Primitive man...assumes that everything is brought about by invisible, arbitrary powers–in other words, that everything is chance. Only he does not call it chance, but intention....Primitive man expects far more of an explanation. What we call pure chance is for him willful intention."[4]

Today the power of reason and causality alone is losing its grip on the modern worldview. We live now in an age of weariness and disillusionment. We have produced bigger and better but at a tremendous cost to the human soul. Technology and scientific advancement are not the enemy. I have tried hard in this book not to fall into that trap. The enemy is the ambitious drive to grab power away from the earth, the dark night of our past and the limitations of our mortality beyond which our reason alone cannot fathom. There is widespread collective anger today overlaying our sense of loss of soul and failed visions. Our corner of the world is having a massive collective nervous breakdown. I confess that in some places in this writing I indicate that this may be for our ultimate good if we survive.

This book is not intended to give a lengthy analysis of how we have gotten to this condition today. At the same time, I could not avoid mentioning how the westernized form of the Christian Church has participated in separating us from the earth and de-souled the individual with its over-rational and literalizing tendency. Sadly, the Church in North America mirrored the persona of the American culture rather than acted as a voice for its collective soul. It too has been seduced by the power of reason and the ability of causality to ease the suffering of the human soul. If we know the reason, almost anything becomes easier to accept. At the same time, I want the reader to clearly know that I am not "against" the Christian paradigm any more than I am against another religion. What I am against is the way it was delivered. The message is not the issue; the medium of the message is. There have been individuals throughout Christian history who have truly given of themselves to make sure that what is meant to be Good News is not Bad News.

There can be no denial, however, that tremendous spiritual damage has been done over most of Christian history throughout the west and wherever that Church went in separating its God from the earth, bringing destruction to those who were close to it, and encouraging its followers to get through their temporal existence as best and as fast as they can to a better world beyond. Earth was not portrayed as our home but as a place to endure, to get through, to be done with. Further, there was no tolerance for the notion of spirits. They were driven away. Matter became inert–dead. It now could be used, shaped and disposed of as we saw fit. In Chapter Two I try to speak of this in the context of the need to redefine the doctrine of the incarnation so that any notion of the kingdom of God will not need to be so separate from either the human race or any aspect of creation itself. I suspect a sharp-shooting theologian could do wonders with this chapter in tearing it down. Frankly, I couldn't really care less, because, whatever would be dismissed, the fact that all creation throughout the cosmic order is interconnected and a living reality can no longer be ignored nor the consequence of this truth for any spiritual construct taken. To accept this can bring us properly into the twenty-first century.

The cultural nervous breakdown we all know so well, the anguish so deeply felt, has another danger: our identification with it in believing that is all there is to it, there is nothing more, there is no way out. Pierre Teilhard de Chardin cautions against two dangers that work against the evolution of life manifesting itself now in the psychical realm carried by the human race: isolation and discouragement. Isolation can manifest itself on either an individual or collective level. Regarding the first he says, "...some innate instinct inclines us to think that to give ourselves full scope we must break away as far as possible from the crowd of others. Is it not in our aloofness from our fellows, or alternatively in their subjection to ourselves, that we will find that 'utmost limit of ourselves' which is our declared goal?"[5] He goes on to show how on a collective level this tendency toward isolation gives rise to "the doctrine of the selection and election of races."[6] Speaking to the second concern, discouragement, he says, "...half a million years, perhaps even a million, were required for life to pass from the prehominids to modern man. Should we now start wringing our hands because, less than two centuries after glimpsing a higher state, modern man is still at loggerheads with himself?...Would not humanity seem to us altogether static if, behind its history, there were not the endless stretch of its prehistory? Similarly...we cannot expect to see the earth transform itself under our eyes in the space of a generation. Let us keep calm and take heart."[7]

The life force demands that we continue to search for direction and clear any path necessary that will bring healing. I believe this is trying to happen in the chaos of our breakdown. In no manner should I be construed to be a fatalist in any aspect of this writing. There is a search for new answers going on today. Even the eruption of the New Age movement, as rootless and sentimental as it can be, is symptomatic of the hunger to find new forms for the spirit to live and ritualize itself. Slowly, concern is being redirected toward earth's preservation. Bookstores are filled with topics related to alternative spiritual forms, matters of ecological concern and analyses of our cultural condition. People are getting more informed of the shadow of our politicians and of politics in general. Though Hollywood continues to remake the hero archetype in thousands of productions, there are signs that this is fading. An example of this is the film "Dances with Wolves," which I have included as a chapter because of its impact on and reflection of the changing American psyche. Here is seen the waning of the dominance of the hero in the life of

Lieutenant Dunbar who, at the beginning of the film, is done with this archetype and now seeks to find his own soul again by connecting with the land as one of its Original People. I present it as an American metaphor descriptive of our wound as well as the direction we need to go in our spiritual renewal.

In Chapter Four I have tried to amplify this same metaphor of our cultural predicament and the needed direction on a personal level. Without doubt it was the most tentative part of this book simply because it reveals specific personal dreams over the course of about ten years. I state there, and again here, that my objective is not to indulge myself but to use these dreams in a more collective manner which is where their final intent lies. No attempt was made to analyze the dreams in all their specifics. It did not seem necessary, and I encourage the reader to be kind in any further interpretations made about my personal psychology.

The most challenging chapter by far was the final one that attempts to describe in a most generalized manner just what the indigenous life is. This is no sophisticated anthropological study but rather an overview based on personal experience, a fair amount of reading, some intuition and a lot of common sense. During this writing I was given a copy of the book *The Two-Million-Year-Old Self* by the Jungian analyst Anthony Stevens.[8] I am both grateful for and encouraged by this book in which he also tries to give definition and experiential life to the indigenous ground of modern people. It was especially interesting to read how he related our rich evolutionary history and our disregard for it to a reconsideration of the psychobiology of symptoms. It is a book well worth reading.

I have titled my own book *Dancing Between Two Worlds,* which admittedly at first carried some personal value because of my involvement in "Indian Country," a feature that can be seen in some of my dreams in Chapter Four. Yet the title carries more than my personal reference. On the more obvious level, it is meant to reflect the required tension of living as a truly modern technological person while remaining conscious of an indigenous life that in no manner needs to possess the earth but desires only to belong more intimately to Her.

To stand between positions opens life to new possibilities. It is a place where one considers a move beyond simple right and wrong, good or bad. Such ethics are easy if that is all there were to it. But when visions, philosophies, and worldviews blend, the matter is not only more problematic but potentially more creative. We want simple answers: I am right and you are wrong! This is good and this is evil! The metaphor of dancing between two worlds expands the reality of our belonging to the universe and encourages other considerations beyond ourselves with its limited point of view. In the history of the human race, we are now unique in our disbelief in spirits and the value of dreams. To dance between two worlds opens again this realm to a partnership with our rational Europeanized inheritance, each ceasing to be the judge of the other which seems so popular today. Both are required for a full appreciation of who we are.

Doing such a dance requires an appreciation of multiplicity. There is more than me or my way, my culture, my race, my religion, my political views, my interpretation of reality. Here we stand with the unknown, that which is "not me," that which is outside myself. Here we have a chance to yield to the bigness beyond ourselves and to the wonderful but significant smallness of our own being. This is not a contradiction any more than was that starry night for me a few years ago. All too frequently there is the temptation to find answers, to break through the unknown, instead of letting ourselves stand the tension of unrevealed possibilities and be worked by what we do not know.

There is a strong tendency in our culture to encourage

and even expect sameness. The greater the difference, the greater the distrust. Perhaps this is not so unusual to people everywhere. But nature is built on the principle of diversity and so is conscious development. We need to differentiate life and to honor that same nature in ourselves that expects diversity. Unfortunately, however, diversity gets replaced by divisiveness. In our own country the battles intensify between Democrats and Republicans, liberal and conservative, left and right. Blame is the ruling paradigm that takes on embarrassing proportions during election times. There is no dancing between worlds here; there is just "my" world. "You" are the enemy. At any given moment we are building an attitude politically that will determine the fundamental issues that will govern our lives. Just how human or mechanical will our species be? Will we respond to the world with a sense of deep community or as compartmentalized masses of people? Will the earth proper be treated and defended as our true home or be disregarded and discarded with little sense of consequence? If we do not make room for the Indigenous One in our political considerations and turn our focus to a global perspective with its shared evolutionary history and yet untold evolutionary future, we will remain with deadened politics that seeks a scapegoat. In fact we are all responsible. In Teilhard de Chardin's words: "...even in the interest of life in general, what is the work of works for man if not to establish, in and by each one of us, an absolutely original centre in which the universe reflects itself in a unique and inimitable way?"[9] It is so difficult to see ourselves as an "original centre" in the context of a cosmic evolutionary history with billions of years behind us. It is hard to see ourselves from such a distance. But the world has now at least seen the earth from outer space, providing some objectivity to remind us of the needed global perspective of who we are, what we have done and what we must yet do. Whether we make the appropriate response will be a matter for history to decide.

What can come out of all this struggle is a more mature spirituality. Throughout this book, I have tried to show how this can only happen by including the earth in our spiritual system. We have suffered our disconnection from the land. Without it, our religion is lifeless and boring. In our hunger we go back to her as well we ought. Like elsewhere we go back also to the original peoples of the land for help. The reader will see the complexity of this issue throughout the book, including the projections made and needing to be withdrawn. I emphasize that we are all indigenous and need to stand alongside the ancestors of this continent, daring finally to listen to what they have to say, to their stories, their sufferings, their worldviews. The Indian culture, spirit and history have been the most suppressed religious sides of the American psyche. At the same time, what are represented here are some of the deepest dimensions of the individual and collective soul. This has given force to the "wannabe" phenomenon so widespread today. I understand this and even have some patience for it because behind it I hear, "I 'wannabe' more truly human, to find my own indigenous root." This is the right direction, though it need not take us to a reservation. The earth is beneath our feet and in our soul. It is here that spiritual renewal will take place.

My own involvement with Native American people has convinced me that they are not by nature against non-Indian people. The distance, reserve and anger often felt are the products of an unresolved ugly history that would make the best of us pull back with caution. At present most tribes are busy just trying to survive in a world that threatens their identity daily. Their anger is real and justified toward anyone who approaches them invasively. At the same time, the hand and heart need to be extended by non-Indian peoples as more frequently than not have been given to us. I recommend genuineness of heart, patience, and keeping one's mouth closed for a while as a good place to start in knowing anyone that seems different from us as well as in knowing our own soul.

At the time of this writing, I have been ceremonially involved with the Brule branch of the Lakota people for eleven years. During this time, I have not only experienced Indian people reach out with their hearts, but I have also seen non-Indian people respond with sincerity, beauty and generosity. How far this will go on a collective level remains to be seen. The Lakota call white people *wasicun*, which has two possible origins: 1. "taker of the fat" (*wasi*=fat, *icu*=take), and 2. "white spirit" (*wa*=white, *sicun*=spirit). These are two potentially different meanings but with one disparaging history. I pray for the day when the name *wasicun* will engender honor, trust and a warm heart for all Indian people.

In conclusion, it is gratitude I feel as I remember all those who have accompanied me these past years and helped give formation to this book. It is risky to name individuals, since often it is someone I hardly know who leaves the needed impression. But specifically I recognize Marlene Whiterabbit Helgemo, Norbert Running, Albert White Hat, Ben Little Bear, Gilly Running, Alberta and Jean Day, Chuck Derby, Joe Moreno, and, with special affection, my brother Florentine Blue Thunder. In my more immediate circles, I am thankful for the "Watertown Dream Group" who read the individual chapters, offering suggestions and encouragement. I am deeply appreciative of the support of Jeff and Therese Grumley who walked much of the same territory that was not always clear, and to the community at Manitoumie, Don and Carole, Frank and Renee, Jim and Sally, who know full well how much healing there is in the land. I thank my good friends Bob Henderson, Dennis Merritt, Harvey Honig, Mary Susan Edwards and Barbara Ferket for their frequent inquiries and support. With both appreciation and affection I extend my thanks to Marjorie Morningstar Millevolte who so graciously and skillfully helped edit this writing and provided some truly wise advice. And to those who gather at the Sacred Lodge, I say, "Pilamayayelo."

Finally, there is Karen, my friend, my partner and my wife, who has walked a few dark trails of her own only to discover her own connection to the stars. She has accompanied me into "Indian Country" and throughout this entire writing. I cannot even imagine what it would have been like to have gone this part of the journey alone. I am proud that she is accepted by the People, performs the ceremonies with both respect and knowledge, and captured the wisdom of years of Sun Dancing. She is truly one who models well what it is to dance between two worlds. Thank you.

Chapter One

Wounded Knee, Wounded Hearts: Our Common Grief

Winding down a path unknown
with souls entwined together
Staying in the dark recesses of the
underworld, waiting patiently
Until that which has been forgotten
can be remembered
And once remembered, can be healed.
Margaret Smerlinski (January 1992)

What lies beneath the landscapes of the American soil, or of any place for that matter, whether it be the wilderness or the countryside or the inner city? We can look anywhere and say "That's beautiful" or "horrible" or "plain." We can see over there a mountain, or here a rock, or there a stream, or yonder a building. But these are only facts of a place. I remember as a child how I and, presumably, most of my classmates would sit and listen to the facts of history–all those names and dates and places to be memorized, kept in order and certainly not confused with one another! After a while, it all seemed to blur together and create a sense of "who really cares anyway?" This would change, however, when on those rare occasions I visited one of those famous historical sites. Here again were these same names, dates and places. Yet what were once only grueling facts were now set in a context, intimately linked together with feeling and soul which can only best be described by the word "story." Facts are not "story." Facts are facts. How do we get to a "story" when we are so caught up in facts–facts that suck the soul out of a person, place or event? We are overwhelmed by facts today that come in the form of an explosion of information, data and statistics. If and how these will be woven together to create the stories that will define our culture is yet to be awaited. In other words, if we have facts, we do not automatically have "story." We just have the material they are made of. Facts alone are a form of materialism. In union with soul, facts become "story."

The landscapes of our own continent hold not just the facts but the memories of a place. In their own mysterious way, they draw out of us the ancient history of our own interior landscapes which are a part of the soil itself. The Land reminds us where we came from and holds the "stories" that dwell within. These stories of the Land have the power of evoking our own personal and collective "stories" we so arrogantly believe that we no longer need. The Land is living and, as such, contains the stories of our long history with it.

Lately, it seems that more and more people are turning their eyes and ears again to these "stories" of the Land of which they themselves are a part. Perhaps this is so because of the exhaustion or depletion of soul out of efforts to live in a fact-finding world coupled with some dim recognition that the only way is to go back to the stage upon which "story" is enacted–the Land itself!

In recent years, I have been taken by a peculiar kind of "story" that acts as a hook deep inside me, against which I cannot break free. The theme of this story is *pathos,* suffering, which soaks the American soil. This is a suffering born in the context of unrecognized and unresolved grief for the violence and destruction done to this land, the original peoples of this land, and consequently and simultaneously to all those who are new to this land in the past five hundred years or so. In other words, everyone has suffered. This suffering is mostly unconscious and lives in the American collective psyche as a force waiting to be reconciled. It is a force that has always acted as a shadow counterpoint to our collective history of opportunism, Manifest Destiny and military victory parades. Most informed people know of such history, but what is not realized is that the force of grief behind it in the end cancels out any "we/they" and "blame/guilt" phenomena. This kind of grief is not just felt a hundred years after an event but at the moment of the event, when the blood is being spilled, when the violence is being done. It is a hidden and silent grief barely visible, pushed aside and buried layer upon layer by the cultural and personal justifications for survival. It is a grief that binds victim and perpetrator in an unconscious alliance. Beyond the hatred, beyond the blame, beyond the guilt is a sense of mutual sharing–namely, that both are victims of a common grief that can only be healed when acknowledged.

The *pathos* of which I speak may best be understood by two of my own dreams. The first came to me about ten years ago:

> I saw, as though I were a bird looking down on the earth, a town as it might have been a century ago. At the same time, I saw an Indian on a horse who had fought a war in this town. I wondered what he wondered. He was on the edge of the community, and I wondered if he were now a statue or landmark. He seemed sad.

From the perspective of a bird, we can understand history, sort the pieces, extract perhaps a new morality based on the lessons of the past. But at the moment of our living, we are not birds; we are humans playing our parts, doing what we know and not always so wisely. From the privileged position of time, we can have a spiritual overview of yesterday's collision of two cultures. The town here is the stereotypic community on the American soil and represents the routine mainstream of American life that had its roots of origin in the need to tame the wilderness and conquer its native dwellers. The Indian was the spiritual custodian of the earth, and it was this one who stood in the way of western expansion, which demanded land ownership by the common person, which in turn supported the notion of free enterprise. This needed to be accomplished by the dominant culture at any price. Even a superficial reading of the history of this process will leave one keenly aware of how bloody and dishonorable it was. This needed to be done even if it meant disrupting the land and relocating thousands of peoples on forced marches to lands unknown to them after illegally seizing their properties. Wiping out vast herds of buffalo, bringing the people to near starvation, and violating promises and treaties were further transgressions.

All of this was not so long ago. To those in the dominant position, it does not seem to matter, for it is as though these occurrences are lost, forgotten, faded in time, and have no consequence today. Feelings do not die on the battlefield or with the passing away of the veterans of those battles. I remember a conference I attended in 1983 on Native American Spirituality where a white clergyman and a Santee Sioux were talking at the dinner table one evening. As they shared themselves, the clergyman said that his great-grandfather had fought against the Sioux people during the New Ulm uprising in Minnesota in 1862. The Santee then responded to his new friend by telling him that his great-grandfather had also fought in that same battle and had been hanged along with thirty-seven others in Mankato, Minnesota. It was the largest legal mass hanging in U.S. history. Now here they were, one hundred and twenty-one years later, trying to make connections across time. It was certainly not so long ago for these two men. There are peoples today on reservations who had grandparents or great-grandparents or known distant relatives who died in such battles and massacres.

So now we can be like a bird and take flight and try to see

from a higher perspective what happened and how we are all affected. The Indian is sad in the dream and is on the edge of the town as only a landmark, perhaps. He was not included in the emergence of American consciousness. For this, everyone has paid a price. That Indian on the edges of the present social structures is that fundamental, indigenous, native "being" in everyone's soul, without which we are all less than human.

The second dream occurred in the early fall of 1990 about four months before the centennial memorial of the Massacre of Wounded Knee to be held on December 29, 1990 at Wounded Knee, South Dakota.

> I dreamed that I was talking with a man about the Massacre of Wounded Knee on December 29, 1890 of which he knew nothing. What I shared was nearly accurate to what I had indeed heard about in waking life. I stated that Chief Big Foot brought his band of Minneconjous to Wounded Knee and turned himself in to the Federal troops. Such surrender was expected as a result of the fear developing in local white settlers over the Ghost Dance that was spreading throughout the Plains. I went on to say that Big Foot and his people turned over their weapons as ordered. No one really knew how the shooting started. An estimated 250 native men, women, and children were mowed down. At this point, I began to cry. I went on to say that on a nearby hill, Hotchkiss guns opened fire. I wept hard and said that I did not realize I had such feeling in me for this event. I related that some wounded crawled to the ravines and died there. I wept harder and said the final tragedy was that the wounded Indians were taken eventually to a church in Pine Ridge for medical treatment because the local hospital was filled with wounded Federal troops. Christmas decorations were still up with a Christmas banner which read "Peace on Earth, Good Will Toward Men." I wept and wept.

Like many people, I can recall places I have visited where

there had been many deaths. I remember very well walking through the Gettysburg battlefield in Virginia and the Dachau concentration camp in Germany, and standing at the Pearl Harbor Memorial over the sunken battleship, Arizona, and more recently before the wailing wall in Washington, D.C., which we have come to know as the Vietnam Memorial. All of these places were awesome in their histories and provoked me to remember that on these sites where people died, they were recognized or honored. The places of these deaths were the result of historical processes bigger than the events themselves. Such places quickly awaken the imagination to so many dying so intensely and evoke a fundamental grief of soul in most of us.

My dream of Wounded Knee shook me with a clarity that few dreams do. It was a dream that took me to a place of too many deaths. It brought an awareness to me of the profound grief lying deep in the American psyche as it is related to the tragic and failed relationship between the dominant culture and the Native American communities. The dream convinced me it had to do with something bigger than my personal psychology. It is true I was informing another part of myself in the dream—trying to raise to consciousness matters that were important to me. But it was not my dream alone. It involved a collective drama that was bigger than my personal story.

For several years I have been involved spiritually with Native American ways through vision quests, sweat lodge ceremonies, the Sun Dance, and as one who respects and uses the sacred pipe. These experiences have given me a glimpse of the beauty and horror of Indian life. I believe that what happened to me through this dream is what happens to many who steep themselves in another's culture, namely, they start responding to the emotional collective history of the people. At one level, as Carl Jung said, the conqueror takes on the attributes of the conquered.

Immigrants and their descendants are in search of a home and are affected by the character of the land and its ancestors. But, on another level, the attitudes and actions one takes toward this land and its original inhabitants affect not only them but oneself. In other words, what we have done to someone else, we have also done to ourselves.

December 29, 1990 marked the centennial year of the Massacre of Wounded Knee. This event itself has become a metaphor for what has happened to all of us. It was not only the final *coup de grace* of the original way of Indian life; it also portrayed the attitudes of five hundred years of Indian/non-Indian relationships. Here was lived out the misunderstandings, the hatred and fear of the unknown, the failed promises, and the indiscriminate killings. If this event were treated like a collective dream, then what is before us is not just a violation against the actual Indian who dwelled upon the American soil, but is also a violation against that same figure who lives in the collective psyche, that indigenous earth-connected side of every person of every nation and religion and is the source of soul and all spiritual attainments. The violence known at Wounded Knee is not just against the Indian people but also against the Indigenous One who lives within us all and from whom we have cut ourselves off. The Indian is a symbol of ourself as an essential person. To kill or repress that side leads to soulless indifference, a condition that seems to afflict our land today. Even the mass burial at Wounded Knee continues the metaphor of how we as a nation have indiscriminately and without regard buried our love and respect for the land, our interconnections to one another and all life, and what it basically means to be a human being, that is, as one who is from the *humus* or soil. With reference to Dee Brown, I say that the non-Indian heart is also buried at Wounded Knee.[10]

To most Americans, the events that happened at Wounded Knee mean little or nothing. Like the man in my dream who did not know, most non-Indian people are unaware of this historical tragedy. What was true of myself in the dream about the unknown but fundamental sadness also lies buried in the collective American psyche. Though many non-Indian people who truly care do feel the sadness, it is usually outweighed by guilt. And with the guilt has often come legitimate but usually illegitimate attempts at reparation. This is an age of guilt and blame. It is the polarity we are in and must live out and outlive. Guilt/blame serves the psyche by raising up a certain level of consciousness that is required to identify ourselves clearly as either victim or perpetrator to begin with. Guilt/blame stirs us up. It awakens us to the violations and brings consciousness to the injustice. We are a guilt/blame society. We go out of our way to avoid, minimize, or deny our complicity. We concentrate our attention on it in such a way that it leaves us consciously immobile and unconsciously resentful. It is true that reparations need to be made for the violations done. Wrongs need to be righted and justice restored. We do need to experience that kind of healing guilt that can bring transformation of consciousness individually and collectively. But even more fundamental and restorative than guilt is sadness–the condition of seeing, admitting and weeping! Sadness certainly can acknowledge the guilt but moves on to the loss behind it. Blame includes one part of the population, guilt another. Grief includes everyone. It is the common element we all share in together and that can join us in the mutual task of finding our way home to the earth. What was unique about my dream was the overwhelming presence of weeping and sadness.

There is a *pathos* in the land today, a suffering that lends itself to pathology. This suffering for the most part lurks in the unknown. It is very real and can best be described as sadness. There is no wailing wall for Wounded Knee or for what it represents–a killing of the collective soul with the killing of the ancestors of this land. And, similarly, there is no place to acknowledge the killing of that same ancestral side of ourselves. As surely as Herod slaughtered the Innocents so long ago, so this also was a slaughter of the Innocents in 1890. It continues to be so within the souls of most members of the dominant culture. But again, this is not about Indians and non-Indians or, as I stated, about "we" and "them" or good guys and bad guys. Everyone played a part. The greater meaning lies deep in the collective psyche at that level where we are all really quite the same. It is here that we have all suffered. Wounded Knee, then, is a metaphor of our own slaughter. Most have been cut off not only from actual Native Americans but from the earth we walk and live upon and the earth we are. I believe this has caused a great deal of inner sadness, perhaps better described as despair, often mistaken for depression. It is a law of the soul that it is impossible to heap such violence on another person or people without simultaneously heaping it on ourselves. Just as a man who beats his wife or girlfriend violates also something basic in himself, so a people who violate the earth and others who dwell on it violate themselves as fellow inhabitants.

In those days before the Massacre, the Ghost Dance was being performed by many of the Indians of the Plains. It was a dance given to the people by the Piute holy man, Wovoka, who told them that if they danced night and day and caused harm to no one and prayed for renewal, the buffalo, along with all their dead relatives, would come back to life. It was believed that Jesus would now come to the Indian people to help them because the white people, whom Jesus first went to, had violated him. This was an attempt to bring about spiritual renewal. It was a dance of regeneration and hope for a disparate people, though it terrified many of the newly arrived settlers through lack of understanding. They thought it was anything but a dance of peace. Too many

Indians dancing with such passion could only lead to one thing: renewed war. The memory of Custer's death was still fresh in their minds, and in addition many of the former hunting bands just did not like agency life. So fear predominated and, with it, the demand for Federal troops to be in the area.

The Indian people, however, just wanted to be left alone to dance and pray and wait for the renewal they believed would surely come if they did everything they were told by the prophet Wovoka. Ghost shirts were worn to protect the Indian from the bullets of the white man. This belief contributed to the tragedy at Wounded Knee. Yet this was a Spirit Dance to bring back the dead and the old way of life that held freedom and meaning and to lift up again a people who had been violated. Though this was a peace dance and was known as such by many in key government positions, it became the reason to bring in the Seventh Calvary, that same unit that was defeated at the Battle of the Little Big Horn fourteen years earlier. Their mission was to keep the peace and round up agitators and promoters of the Ghost Dance, one of whom was Chief Big Foot.

I do not know what all awaits us post-1990, but I do know an opportunity for renewal and regeneration is before us all. For four consecutive years, present-day riders had honored the two week journey to Wounded Knee which Big Foot and his band took then, enduring terribly cold weather and hardship. But, as of 1990, these two week memorial Big Foot rides have ended. The spirits of those slain can now finally rest after one hundred years. The politicians have spoken. The ceremonies are over. Yet it seems there is still a "dance" needing to be done. It seems that even today our souls wish, through some desperate Spirit Dance attempt of our own, to recover the past as the place of origin. This is not a regressive impulse but one sought for the sake of renewal. Such a "dance" is one of the heart and soul and, as such, is capable of pushing humankind forward not as an enemy of the earth or of one another but as ones who have again found a rightful place alongside the rest of creation.

Perhaps we could, in our own ways, imagine such a Spirit Dance today for all peoples to remember the dead, to pray for a new day, to weep fully and, with their tears, to cleanse the way for a new creative order on our soil. Such a "Dance" would not be for the sake of bringing back the old days but for inviting back a relationship to our own ancestral depths that are so very much connected to the earth. Such a "Dance" of heart and soul will call out for the return of our own *indigenous nature,* which has long been banished in the name of cultural and technological advancement, so that this nature will once again be respected and heard in both the personal and the collective realms.

What was so historically literalized in the Ghost Dance years ago and culminated in the tragedy of Wounded Knee can today take on symbolic value psychologically and spiritually. The continuous dancing in the circle of wholeness to bring peace and renewal to the earth, plus reimagining the Jesus mythos along indigenous lines, might indeed be helpful to all of us regardless of our cultural or religious orientation. In other words, we must continue attempts to remain conscious of our intimate and delicate relationship to all creation. We must rethink the religious attitudes of our culture that have kept us separated from ourselves and the earth. Our faithfulness to this struggle, all together, makes the Dance. The Ghost shirts did not protect the people in those days, but what they represented is a fundamental truth. Painted on these garments were pictures of the sun and moon and stars, thus raising the moment of renewal to a cosmic level. Such a perspective is desperately needed in our times. We human beings or two-leggeds are not the dominators of this earth or the universe in which it is contained. Rather we are fellow citizens and relationally mothers, fathers, daughters and sons, sisters and brothers with the rest of creation. We can once again try to see the world not just as fact but also as metaphor. Then the river, the tree, the stone, the mountain, and all the creatures we can imagine are our relatives. This is not poetry that we can muse over and put aside; it is an ecological imperative and simply good physics. If we can but see this and hold this in our heart, then we are like one who has come home. That we have not yet is our sadness.

Shortly after I had my dream, a friend of mine responded to it with a fantasy. He said that like the Vietnam Memorial, we should have another wailing wall recognizing the casualties of the long history of Indian and non-Indian peoples. Such a wall would list the names of all the broken treaties, all the massacres and wanton killings, all the properties violated, and all the sacred objects desecrated. Such a wall would not be there to invoke blame but to raise up and make conscious a side of history that has affected everyone. His fantasy is a reminder of the need for collective recognition of what has happened and, like the Vietnam Memorial, still stirs in us beyond the layer of blame and guilt. Such a wall, literally or in our hearts, would help us remember and weep so that healing may come. It may even invoke the spirits of old to look our way again so that we collectively may be strengthened to truly bring about "Peace on Earth, Good Will Toward All Humanity."

Chapter Two

A Matter of Incarnation, or "Do You Believe in Spirits?"

Grandmother, and great Mother Earth,
upon You the people will walk;
may they follow the sacred path with Light,
not with the darkness of ignorance.
May they always remember their relatives at the four quarters,
and may they know that they are related
to all that moves upon the universe....
Black Elk[11]

Some words are like an event, a happening that will not go away. His were like that. "Do you believe in spirits?" he asked me. He was a Lakota Sioux, originally from South Dakota, a solid traditionalist and, at the same time, western trained as an Episcopal priest. He was a sensitive and caring man who had struggled his way to a position of balancing two worlds. We both had just returned from what is more commonly known as a "vision quest" and were resting now in the ceremonial lodge talking late into the night. Strange things had happened to both of us, so his question, though appropriate, took me off-guard. If he had asked me whether I believe in archetypes or complexes, well, that would have been easy. "Of course," I would have said. "Without a doubt." However, "spirits" seemed to take things to a different level. My own initial silence to the question bothered me, since, after all, I had also studied for the clergy, but never once in the seminary had we talked about spirits. I was on my own with this one. So finally I answered, "Yes, I do believe in spirits, but I do not always know how they manifest themselves."

A few years have gone by since that event, but I still hold to my answer. Where are the spirits nowadays, and do we have the eyes and ears to see and hear them? I, like many others in our times, have mostly kept quiet about these matters, believing the Christian community would say it really was not Christian enough, and the Jungian community would think I had a complex of some kind. Perhaps so, but it seems bigger than this. Whether we speak of angels, archangels, complexes, archetypes or spirits is a matter of culture or personal choice. In varying ways, the resistance to such words seems to involve an attitude in the western world that is driven to find answers to everything and to distrust that which we cannot see or explain. It involves a collective need to both literalize and personalize the soul and its journey to such an extent that attempts to talk about such matters from the constructs of depth psychology or religion become suspect. The end result is often a detached indifference on the one hand or a literalized fundamentalism on the other. In either case, the question of whether spirits exist at all need never be addressed.

My own point of view is to see people as intrinsically religious and to view our basest and noblest adventures throughout life from this perspective.[12] I have been affected by three cosmologies: the Judeo-Christian, the Lakota Sioux and the scientific. Each has been a source of balance to the other and together have opened perspectives for me I do not believe I would otherwise have gotten. Yet coming to this has not been by a straight line. These cosmologies have forced questions that do not belong to me alone. When I imagine the Judeo-Christian world of North America today, I see a suffering rising from a spiritually anemic condition that is causing sadness and anger in a growing number of people. These are people who can no longer force themselves to go to the temples and sanctuaries. At the same time, they cannot bring themselves to entirely leave them either. It is an anemia that is alienating our youth and leaving them bored liturgically and theologically. It does not take much to recognize the general spiritual malaise, the dispiritedness in both the Protestant and Catholic worlds today. A sickness of soul does prevail. The disturbance crosses denominational lines and raises the question whether the traditional divisions in Christiandom–that is, Roman, Eastern, Anglican Catholic from the Protestant world, generally–are entirely accurate anymore. It is as if a new spiritual struggle has emerged today that transects denominational preferences and includes all who would seek change and renewal and together strive against any aspect of the American persona that would stand in the way of compassion, justice and creativity.

This spiritual struggle is to be seen today in the suffering of the people and the land. We have seen how far this suffering has gone in the lethal explosion of the drug world, in general anxiety and despair, in the mass of wounded children crowding the psychotherapists' offices, in our elders who do not feel connected or useful anymore, in the sandwich generation who are asking more and more today, "Just what is it all about anyway?" and, finally, in the earth-ness of the body we are and the body of the earth we are a part of.

There are no simple answers or solutions to this vast network of collective suffering we are experiencing today. But I do believe it is connected to the spiritual attitudes or lack of them in our times. It is interesting to me that Christendom holds within its belief structure at least one perspective that can assist in its own renewal and act as a challenge to the culture. This lies in its doctrine of the incarnation. This particular doctrine holds that God took on flesh and became human, that divinity entered into union with matter in such a way that God became more approachable and humankind more elevated. For Christendom, this focused in Jesus of

Nazareth who became the prototype of union between God and humankind. The problem developed, however, when this Jesus of Nazareth as the Incarnation of God would himself become the gatekeeper for the damned and justified. This literalized and blocked a more profound truth: that inherent in the human soul is the reality of God, however conceived, and that dignity and honor, as a result of the divine presence within each of us, are givens. With such a perspective, the human race could then participate as a partner with God in the creative endeavor. To emphasize a literal approach to theology tends to weaken the creative and imaginative dimension of the soul and can produce an attitude and behavior that are too black and white. The result can be that what was meant to be Good News far too often became Bad News, which itself was the result of a narrow and literal understanding of the notion of incarnation. Incarnation means much more. Jesus of Nazareth himself knew this when he stated, "Truly, truly, I say to you, before Abraham was, I am" (Jn 8:58), meaning that what he represents goes back to the beginning of time. He himself did not mean for the human race to lock into some literalized view of who he was as he suggests when he also said, "Far greater things than this will you see." Thus, with open hearts and minds we can be led to see that behind his incarnation is a greater meaning that is related to the mystical union of Spirit and Matter, Divinity and Humankind, in short, to a dynamic unfolding of incarnation in all of life. In other words, the incarnation in Jesus was not even for humankind alone but for all of creation.

This battle between Spirit and Nature has been of immense proportions throughout most of Christian history. Concerning this conflict, Jung says, " 'Spirit' is one aspect, 'Nature' another. 'You may pitch Nature out with a fork, yet she'll always come back again,' says the poet (Horace). Nature must not win the game, but she cannot lose. And whenever the conscious mind clings to hard and fast concepts and gets caught in its own rules and regulations–as is unavoidable and of the essence of civilized consciousness–nature pops up with her inescapable demands. Nature is not matter only, she is also spirit. Were that not so, the only source of spirit would be human reason" ("Paracelsus as a Spiritual Phenomenon" [1942], in Collected Works 13: *Alchemical Studies*, 1967). That "nature...is also spirit" has been difficult for the western Christian Church to grasp. Yet, in its greatest sense, the notion of the incarnation would mean the full embodiment of the Spirit of Life in the full Matter of Things.

Such perspectives are contradictory to western thought and thus fall into the realm of shadow, that is, what we do not know and thus may even fear or decry as evil. For the most part, matter has been seen as dead, without life, waiting to be used in whatsoever way we can. It is easier this way, for then we can place ourselves outside the complex web of inter-relationships that the earth as our Mother provides. To the indigenous mind, the earth is a living Mother that holds us all in unity. To see Her as dead disembodies our spirituality and places humankind at the center of the universe which leads, by matter of fact, to an anthropocentric view of life. This is to say that all of life takes on value only by how it is seen in relationship and benefit to humankind. We will forever war to determine whose anthropocentric view is most valid. Meanwhile the earth and all its inhabitants suffer.

A clear example of life seen in other than anthropocentric terms came in the form of a dream I had several years ago:

> I was at a resort for a weekend retreat. A few of us were gathered in an elegant room for hors d'oeuvres and conversation. I was with a woman when two men came in and began to engage me with questions of a complicated nature. One

in particular carried on the discussion which became quite philosophic and was designed to trap me. It was about the vast difference between the natural world and people. I now became convinced of my own view and referred to a large tree outside through the windows of this room. I asked, "Is that tree alive?" He answered, "Yes." I asked if he was alive, and, if alive, did he have a soul? Again he said, "Yes." Then I said, "If you are alive and, because of this, have a soul, and the tree is alive, does it not mean that the tree has a soul also?" He said, "I guess a little bit." I replied, "That 'little bit' is what you must now think on." I had outmaneuvered his attempt to get me, and I walked away with the woman quite pleased with myself.

This dream reflects the struggle of most people in general today. The debate in the dream challenges the notion that humankind is not a part of the natural order of things and, conversely, the natural order does not include humankind. Such a view separates us from the ecosystem, viewing it as one would an aquarium from the outside rather than seeing ourselves as vitally linked to it. If we go wrong, it goes wrong and vice versa. Jung states, "Without soul, spirit is dead as matter, because both are artificial abstractions; whereas man originally regarded spirit as a volatile body, and matter as not lacking in soul" (Commentary by C.G. Jung in CW 13: *Alchemical Studies,* 1967 to Richard Wilhelm's *The Secret of the Golden Flower*).

Shortly after this dream, a similar one came:

I was with a man and woman I know who are quite fundamentalistic. During our discussion, she raised the question, "How is Christ in it?" I felt her critical attitude and picked up an object that a laborer had made with his hands from a factory. I asked her if this man had put such care and love and his own soul into the making of that product, was not God expressing Himself through that man? She said, "Yes." I then asked, "If Christ is in that man, would not Christ also be in that product?" She answered affirmatively.

Though the logic is not tight, the point remains that the unconscious of both myself and the industrial age we live in is trying to help the fundamentally rationalized mind to reclaim a view of the sacredness of all things. It is easy for the modern mind to pretend a distance from nature and hold to an anthropocentric point of view and the distorted spirituality that goes with it. But there is no spirituality of any worth that is not connected to the earth. Some price will be paid at some level both within ourselves and in the body of the earth itself for turning our backs on this reality. About this Jung says:

> The Platonic freedom of the spirit does not make a whole judgment possible; it wrenches the light half of the picture away from the dark half. This freedom is to a large extent a phenomenon of civilization, the lofty preoccupation of that fortunate Athenian whose lot it was not be born a slave. We can only rise above nature if somebody else carries the weight of the earth for us. The dark weight of the earth must enter into the picture of the whole ("A Psychological Approach to the Dogma of the Trinity, 1942/48," in Collected Works 11, *Psychology and Religion: West and East, 1958/1969).*

Because the western world generally has, by its denial of the earth as a living entity, turned its back on the "dark weight of the earth," others of lesser circumstance have been forced through projection to carry the earth for us. These have usually been indigenous peoples, people of color, women or our own diseased bodies. All have taken their blows in our attempts to keep the idea of matter incarnate from our theological and psychological doorsteps. It is presumed in the west that matter is evil or, at best, somewhere between evil and good, thus requiring others to carry the dark weight of the earth for us. This is easier to see theologically from the perspective of our two thousand year history, but psychologically is this split true in our times? Indeed it is. For the most part, modern psychology sees *psyche* as confined to the limits of ego with its personalized history and adaptational problems. There is little recognition of one's personal soul being related to a world soul or having or needing a relationship to the earth. Western psychology has not yet embraced the idea that most of our psychotherapeutic ills are direct consequences of being separated from a living environment conceived as home.

Matter *is* living. This is not inconsistent with the discoveries of modern physics. With this view, all of matter is in motion, vital with energy and part of a system of force fields that link any given aspect of matter with the entire cosmos, challenging the mind to open itself to a vast understanding of inclusiveness and unity. The notion of incarnation must include these two principles so that the entire cosmic landscape can be seen as one ecosystem providing the mind and the imagination with a chance to see this wonder in a tiny particle of matter and to see matter in the fullness of this wonder.

There is an astonishing lack of imagination today in seeing God in the matter of things. Western religion generally speaking does not make much reference to the presence of a Cosmic Christ in the "matter" of creation. Protestantism especially has suffered the loss of awareness of the mystical in the moment of our living. Without a sense of the mystical it is difficult to have the eyes and ears to move beyond the literal which, all too easily, leads to a path of limiting parochialism. This parochial exclusivity of Christian salvation produces an unintended shadow problem of judgmentalism and power over people and weakens its primary message of compassion. There is a loss of incarnational spirituality for most people of the western world that has been governed, for the most part, by patriarchal systems. It is sad that the notion of "patriarchal" has taken on such negative tones in our times. Yet this is so only because of an imbalance of the masculine archetype that has resulted in the devaluing of the feminine principle. Our psychological energy has been solar, upward, sky and spirit directed in contrast to lunar, downward, earth and nature directed. This simple formula is the reason why the concept of incarnation has not fared well in this corner of the world. In Taoist language, Yang has ruled; Yin has been in decline. All have suffered the weight of this imbalance. For this reason the lack of the feminine is not just a women's problem but the problem of our entire culture.

A good example of the inclusivity of this problem is seen in the dream of a thirty-eight year old man:

> I'm talking with a group of church people (like a committee) which seems like some kind of an interview, like the Senate confirmation hearings. I'm discussing something about being with a male friend. I tell them we talked about the situation under consideration as a "male problem" caused by a "male church." One woman on my left asks me about it again. I get irritated and repeat what I just said about recognizing the problem as a "male problem."

Granting that this dream deals with this man's own personal male issues, it also places them in the context of a collective setting, namely, a "male church" which is a problem for all of us. It is not just that men literally have been in positions of authority and power, but that patriarchal attitudes and approaches to life have dominated even the men as this dream suggests. The dream even suggests it is not enough to explain this problem just in relationship to the feminine and what it has done to women. The dreamer gets irritated at this and repeats that there is indeed a male problem caused by a male religious point of view. It may be that women generally, like indigenous people, are more in touch consciously with the loss of incarnational attitudes, staying in touch with the immediacy of life and furthering relationships. Nevertheless, we should hold no sentiments here, for the viciousness of a patriarchy out-of-control can manifest itself just as easily through women simply because we are all under the umbrella of a masculine archetype that is not in proper relationship with the feminine. It is not enough to just have the feminine archetype return. It must return in a balanced relationship with the masculine. This union is a part of the fundamental core of each human being which has been from the beginning. It remains basic to what I have referred to repeatedly as the "indigenous" perspective of life we have all inherited. It was no accident that with the rise of the patriarchy, not only the feminine side of life would go into decline and hiding but any connection to our indigenous past would be held down or cut off along with those peoples who hold to this way of life. Since "indigenous" means "to be born from within" (Gk. *genes*=one born, *indu*=within), to lose our connection to this past means to lose any sense of our earth as the womb and home that brought us into being. Meanwhile, matter, in a sense, becomes a forgotten "relative." The stage is set for a non-incarnational view that strips soul from the earth. So we wonder why we despair and why violence is so easy!

"To be born from within" is important for an understanding of incarnation that does not lead to separatism. The noted French paleontologist, Pierre Teilhard de Chardin, in his previously cited book, *The Phenomenon of Man,* traces the evolutionary unfolding process of our planet with the first molecule, giving way to the first cell and then to the expansion of the universe itself. The conditions of everything that now exists, including human consciousness, were already there at the beginning. In his own words:

> It is impossible to deny that, deep within ourselves, an "interior" appears at the heart of beings, as it were seen through a rent. This is enough to ensure that, in one degree or another, this "interior" should obtrude itself as existing everywhere in nature from all time. Since the stuff of the universe has an inner aspect at one point of itself, there is necessarily a double aspect to its structure...co-extensive with their Without, there is a Within to things (p. 56).

Later he states:

> To write the true natural history of the world, we should need to be able to follow it from *within*. It would thus appear...as an ascension of inner sap spreading out in a forest of consolidated instincts. Right at its base, the living world is constituted by consciousness clothed in flesh and bone. From the biosphere to the species is nothing but an immense ramification of psychism seeking for itself through different forms (p. 151).

That the "stuff of the universe has an inner aspect" and, from the beginning, held a "psychism seeking for itself through different forms" became increasingly difficult to accept as this "psychism" manifested itself in the *human* branch of the evolutionary tree. Our consciousness has exploded into increasingly complex forms but, simultaneously, we have become unconscious of the inherent consciousness of the natural world. Western Christianity does not do well with this notion because of its tendency toward literalization. To think eucharistically, for example, of the body and blood of Christ, which is the "stuff" of the universe, as not being other than literal bread and wine misses the depth of this sacrament that insists on making its altar in every atom, molecule and cell.

Chardin, in one of his great moments as both scientist and priest, plunged his understanding of this sacrament into the heart of matter itself. On one of his scientific expeditions, he wanted to celebrate the Mass but had neither bread nor wine. He writes:

> Since once again, Lord—though this time not in the forests of the Aisne but in the steppes of Asia—I have neither bread, nor wine, nor altar, I will raise myself beyond these symbols, up to the pure majesty of the real itself; I, your priest, will make the whole earth my altar and on it will offer you all the labours and sufferings of the world (*Hymn of the Universe,* New York and Evanston: Harper and Row, 1961).

How we view the notion of incarnation is a most important issue for the western world, and it moves beyond solely Christian definitions. It is an issue for everyone insofar as we need to rethink, reimagine and reclaim a living relationship to a living earth. It is also important because what view we take determines how we will place ourselves in the creative structure and what value we give to creation and ourselves as part of it. It is important because it determines the limits of how sacred or unholy we believe matter to be, how at home on the earth we feel, and how ethically committed we are to healing the suffering of the earth.

If the land is living, and if we truly know it to be so, we would treat it carefully, responsibly and compassionately. If the earth is like our Mother, if this is more than a New Age sentiment or fantasy, then we would never treat Her as we do. As one very spiritually tired man told me years ago, "If I could only let myself do what I needed to do, I would get down and hug the earth."

It is time to do just that and return in remembrance to that from which we came. We have forgotten our origins. The "whence" of our being makes little sense in a world that clutters our lives with priorities that have little to do with soul making. The speed limit has been lifted and our lives are moving faster than ever in some direction in which we are not even sure. Remembering our origins is not some regressive move but a regrounding in and a remembering of the essentials of who we are.

Creation stories do not mean much to most people today. Yet they existed and continue to exist in the liturgies of religions throughout the world. In most Native American communities, they are re-enacted in the rite of purification involving a purification (sweat) lodge, fire, water and heated rocks. Entering the half-domed lodge approximates a return to the primordial beginnings. This humble structure of canvas cover and willow frame becomes the universe in its totality. Recognizing this, one says (in the Sioux tradition), "all my relatives," when entering and leaving, thus acknowledging one's relationship to all things in the universe. It becomes a sacred place where *micro* and *macro* reflect each other. In the center is a shallow pit into which red hot rocks are brought one at a time from the sacred fire. A bucket of water is brought in and the door opening is closed. Now there is only darkness embracing the red glow of the rocks. Time stops, space changes. The universe is there for you and all your relatives in the creative order, all sitting in a circle with no beginning or end, all of equal status. It becomes now the beginning of time when there was just darkness and then fire and water. We are brought back to our beginnings where now cleansing and renewal can take place. When we have some reminder of where we came from, we can remember better who we are. That is the cleansing. Fire and water from the sacred center of the lodge (universe) are the two opposites merging to form steam, which is conceived now as the breath of *Wakan Tanka,* the Great Mystery or Unknown. The European mind moves from left brain to right brain to no brain to that letting go of conceptions and misconceptions where something can once again happen. It becomes a creation story of renewal for many now, of a return to perspective, that is to say, to a better sense of one's place in the total schema of life. Concerns are better ordered, the lowly are brought up and the lofty are brought down. Sometimes healing occurs and visions are received. Most often an inner peace and strength are regained. Here in the darkness and in the beginning of things, differences of race, class, education, age and gender weaken. When I sit in purification lodges, I do not feel white or red, young or old, but ancient. It is the place where I touch and am touched by the "Ancient One" *(Tunkashila)*. It becomes a place where we all are reminded of our unity to one another. The purification ceremony does powerful things because of the Native American understanding of incarnation as knowing all of creation as alive, endowed with energy and related to everything else. Everything, according to the Lakota Sioux, has *skan,* a vital energy presence that moves all things in the universe. It is like the Great Mystery or the Unknown moving in all things. Nothing is dead.

If we look at the incarnation as the entire universe being an embodiment of the Spirit, however conceived, then let us think and feel on a more cosmic level even when we look in the stranger's eye. I remember once dreaming:

> I was praying and then for just a short moment realized I was praying in a cosmic way, i.e., that I was aware of the cosmos as my backdrop to my prayer. I thought that that was the way my prayers were to be all the time.

"For just a short moment" is just another way of saying how difficult it is to get out of the narrow frame of viewing life and the sacred. It is important to view the sacred communications of prayer from this cosmic "backdrop."

Jung is the leading psychologist of our times who has documented and given some definition to the cosmic dimension of the human psyche. With his understanding of the collective unconscious, the human soul has been elevated to a position of dignity simply because of its rootedness in primordial history. The history of the universe is coded into the psychic structure of each of us. No longer is our unconscious just ours alone but is rather shared with all people beyond the layers of our personal histories and with all life at its deepest. To descend to our deepest layers is to go all the way back to the Big Bang that is now the scientific myth of creation uniting all peoples the universe over. Our modern consciousness would like to believe that all there is to the psyche is what we know about it. To suggest an unknown layer of the psyche that is older and wiser than our limited ego consciousness would be to admit to an unpredictable and capricious quality to life, a fact few moderns can tolerate.

Jung describes it this way:

> The life of the psyche is the life of mankind. Welling up from the depths of the unconscious, its springs gush forth from the root of the whole human race...(CW 5, *Symbols of Transformation,* p. 202).

> The psyche is not of today; its ancestry goes back many millions of years. Individual consciousness is only the flower and the fruit of a season, sprung from the perennial rhizome beneath the earth; and it would find itself in better accord with the truth if it took the existence of the rhizome into its calculations. For the root matter is the mother of all things (*Ibid.*, p. xxiv).

> I can only gaze with wonder and awe at the depths and heights of our psychic nature. Its non-spatial universe conceals an untold abundance of images that have accumulated over millions of years of living development and become fixed in the organism (*Memories, Dreams, and Reflections,* edited by Aniela Jaffe, New York: Vintage Books, 1963, p. 399).

St. Paul put it this way:

> For the creation waits with eager longing for the revealing of the sons of God....We know that the whole creation has been groaning in travail together until now; and not only the creation, but we ourselves (Rom 8:19, 22–23a).

So again this seems to be what a full understanding of incarnation ought to be about, namely an embrace of Matter and Spirit from the furthest galaxies down to the sub-atomic levels of life. However this is described, scientifically or religiously, life is best understood and most satisfied when accepted within the total frame of both organic and inorganic realities. Nothing less than this is adequate to be called incarnational.

But now we return to where we started regarding this matter of spirits. Whether they exist or not is for each of us to ponder. Do you believe in spirits? Such a question makes fun of reductionist thinking and tames the mind that wants everything in its place. There is no room for literalism, materialism or dead matter here. With this question, all things come potentially alive, all things have voice, intention, direction and reaction. With it, the earth becomes a living being, truly incarnational in the fullest sense, reminding us of our aboriginal roots that are far more open to unknown possibilities. Perhaps the question itself, if nothing else, gives a frame to our quest to realign with the earth and our indigenous bond to it from a religious point of view.

Chapter Three

The Collective Search: An American Metaphor, "Dances with Wolves"

I think this white man is probably lost.
Wind in His Hair

I was just thinking that of all the trails in this life, there is one that matters more than all the others. It is the trail of a true human being. I think you are on this trail, and it is good to see.
Kicking Bird (from the film, "Dances with Wolves")

The quest to realign with the earth in a more incarnational manner is always easier for individuals than nations. Yet there are indications in our times that the western world is slowly making its way back to the earth or at least reconsidering its relationship to the land as something more than just to be used. One of the remarkable cultural expressions of this quest is Kevin Costner's film "Dances with Wolves." Seldom does a film impact a nation as this one did when it made its debut in 1990. Often it is not whether one has seen the film, but "how many times." The beauty and fascination of this story have held the American psyche not because it presents just one more adventure, but because it is a living metaphor of discovery of self, of a journey back to find those roots common to all human beings. It touches our longing for individuation but this time in the context of finding again the earth as home and the Indigenous One as an essential but forgotten aspect of our own identity.

North America has now passed the five hundredth year since Christopher Columbus landed on this continent. Looking back over this span of time, there are many in our country who would say this is nothing to celebrate because it marked the beginning of an horrendous holocaust that continues to this day. Of all the ethnic groups in our country that suffer injustice in our day, the Native Americans are the most neglected. The suffering of these people is the least understood, the least defined, and has evoked the least response from our nation as a whole. There are reasons for this, and I believe this film touches on some of them.

Today the Indian communities are joined by many non-Indian peoples who share the indignation at what has happened in our long history together. There is a growing demand for justice felt on both sides. But in addition to this, and less clear, is a subtle awareness that this long history is "our" history "together," and that we share in common a deep grief, a collective suffering if even on an unconscious level for what has been done. This is shrouded in anger and blame and the response of denial or guilt. But then we know that the alternative to facing our true suffering and deep grief is to deny it and substitute it with an inflated use of power, arrogance and brutality.

I wish to approach this film, as one would any good story, with the respect due to it, pointing out as one would on a long walk the beautiful flowers, trees, or rocks encountered along the way, knowing that each of them is part of the walk itself. "Dances with Wolves" has now taken its place as a collective story, an American metaphor, and, as such, serves as a base for comment and reflection about where we are as a people, Indian and non-Indian alike. Finally, if we are willing, it will challenge us to redefine our attitude and resolve as we move further on from that year of accountability, 1992, and move into the third millennium.

"Dances with Wolves" can be taken on both a personal

and a collective level, that is, as though it were one's own story or the story of our nation. Both work. In other words, if we understood the entire film as a dream, our dream or the dream of our culture, then everything that happens in the story can be taken as an aspect of ourselves or the culture we live in. It does not matter then if one is Indian or non-Indian, male or female, urbanite or pure naturalist in a mountain hut. All aspects of the story are reflections of ourself and the times we live in. This is the symbolic approach that takes us beyond the literal events and people into the world of meaning and transformation.

There are many scenes people talk about that have touched them deeply in this symbolic way, that say more about them/us than the particular scene itself. Some of the most common are the suicide run of Lieutenant Dunbar in the beginning, Major Fambrough's odd behavior, Wind in His Hair crying out in anger at Dunbar in the beginning and in pain for his departure at the end, the buffalo hunt, Dunbar's private dance around his own fire and the killing of his horse, Cisco, and his wolf companion, Two Socks. But, structurally, the best place to begin is at the beginning.

BEYOND THE HERO OR THE LETTING GO

The movie version begins with Lieutenant Dunbar lying on a surgeon's table after a Civil War battle, severely wounded in his foot. An amputation is imminent. But foregoing an amputation, he would rather die and sets off on a suicide run across a stalemated field held on one side by the Union army and on the other by the Confederates. That was the micro-moment of a nation against itself or of those moments in one's own life where we are faced with alternatives that are pitiable and have the feel of too much loss no matter which way we turn. It is the place of the hero with nowhere to go and is reminiscent of Achilles of old. He too was wounded in the foot, that most vulnerable place of the hero, since it is upon this that he or she stands in the attempt to provide a position of moral justice, however ill conceived, to do what needs to be done. It is here we feel the weight of our convictions that have the power to determine what we live or die for. But when this is to be taken away–amputated–when what we have stood for, ordered our lives around and drew our identities from is shot out from underneath us, the result can go all the way from bitterness and rage to apathy and depression. Dunbar chose neither of these. He chose instead to step out of the senseless killing on either side and submit himself to the ultimate letting go. Here he was playing by a different set of rules than the established heroic military mind. In a Christ-like gesture of extended arms on a horse carrying him to a sure death, he gives himself over. It was a "Father, into Thy hands I commend my spirit" moment. In the language of the soul, it was the moment of recognizing that what we have so valued and placed as our foundation is now gone. The mortal wound to the foot is often the necessary wound that demands letting go of our life as we know it. Such a submission is required if any change or transformation is to take place.

The uniqueness of this film is that it breaks the pattern of what is expected of heroes. Most recount an entire story just to establish the hero. "Dances with Wolves" begins with the breakdown of the hero and shows the hero as tired and unwilling to assume this role any longer. Ironically, however, Dunbar does not die, and in his own words says, "The strangeness of this life cannot be measured. In trying to produce my own death, I was elevated to the status of a living hero." He was brought back to where he started, to the place of hero, but now it did not matter. The death he sought was not only his own but also the death of his wish to be the hero. His statement is a good reminder for those times when, being required to let go for the sake of our own individuation, our soul is prepared to elevate us to the status of a true human being.

In our own times, the hero as the dominant archetype is in decline. Since the 1960s the shadow of the hero that is often expressed in the misuse of power has been exposed in politics, religion, and across the professions. The place of the hero is important in the evolution of consciousness and in itself provides no threat. What is damaging is the fixation on the hero/heroine with the resulting inflation that uses power not in the service of cultural development but as a dominating crippling force over it. We are all responsible for this because collectively we have demanded heroes/heroines. When they let us down, we take them down, often with dramatic force and public embarrassment. But the cycle of resurrecting new heroes will go on until we become aware that it is mostly a matter of projecting onto them our own unlived heroic nature that is meant to be in the service of individuation. Heroes/heroines are meant to help usher in a new consciousness, a new way of being and thinking with all the imagination and courage that such require. Once that is accomplished, it is just as well that they slip away quietly and join the rest of the human race, at least in attitude and demeanor.

On a personal level the hero/heroine often begins to wane during mid-life. What was once required to even get a person into life in the first place is now an interference to further development. Mid-life becomes a crisis to the hero/heroine, but to the rest of the psyche it is an opportunity. This is the time when our values and ethics change. What we have held so dear for so long does not seem to matter so much anymore. The convictions that served us so well turn flat and might now even amuse us. The hero/heroine is in decline. But perhaps it is more accurate to say that the last act of the hero/heroine is now required, that is, to imagine beyond itself, to let go of what it has accomplished and turn into the unknown in a gesture of letting go. Metaphorically, this was Lieutenant Dunbar racing across the battlefield in what he thought was his last moment of surrender. It proved to be a transformative event that forced him in a direction away from the military mind and the existing battle to the unknown edges of his life—the place of the frontier.

THE FRONTIER OR "BEYOND HERE BE DRAGONS"

With the death of the hero, it was fitting that Dunbar wanted to go to the frontier. The frontier marks the outer edge of the known civilized world. It is the meeting place of the known and unknown. Here is where one comes to the limits of the old ways that often try to hang on, especially now, in a compulsive manner, or at other times will just wait around to see what happens, or perhaps yield to the unknown and enter it. This is the in-between place, the transition moment that can produce the hysterical reflex of terror and disorientation because one is stuck there, or it can become the crossing-over place into a new awareness of life and self. In any event, it is the place where, like Dunbar, one says of one's life, "I cannot go back to the battling, the senseless killings of a culture (person) at war with itself (himself/herself), but I do not know what awaits me." It is the place of Major Fambrough and Fort Sedgewick.

This is a most peculiar part of the story, giving an impression that it does not fit. Yet it remained in both the movie and book version of "Dances with Wolves." Major Fambrough is portrayed as a man who has gone crazy. He lives in the fantasy of the Arthurian Court with himself as king ruling over his subjects—Dunbar being one of them. He drinks too much, has lost orientation, and has basically become psychotic. Though he rules with a fantasy of ultimate power, he cannot even control his simple bodily functions: "I pissed in my pants and no one can help me." He is pathetically helpless and ineffectual.

Fambrough represents anyone or any part of ourselves on the edge of two opposing realities. When a bridge is being built between two quite different cultures or between two oppositional and tension-laden points within ourselves, that same bridge can be either the means of crossing from one to the other, or it can be the place from which we jump into insanity. It is not easy to shift cultural paradigms. To move, for example, from one political or religious worldview to another can be quite unnerving and confusing. It can cause a counter-action of falling even deeper into the familiar and predictable way of doing and looking at life. This results in a dogmatic and fundamentalistic worldview which is a form of inflation that sets an individual or people up as always being right. Major Fambrough represents that part of any of us or any part of our culture that has pulled away from the familiar ground, the accepted collective standards, but has not found a psychological net to land in that will give new creative definition to who one is.

Fambrough's life had reached the place of a worn-out inflation that leads to madness and senselessness. He is that side of ourselves or our culture that shoots itself in the foot or pisses in its pants in its attempt to stay on top, not even knowing its soul is gone. There is a relationship between him and Dunbar in that they both attempt suicide, but where Dunbar failed, Fambrough succeeds. He is the old value system just simply wearing out and represents that side of our culture today that is losing its grip. The dominant patriarchal hold is breaking down, resulting in a collective disorientation and scrambling for new definitions of how to live sanely and authentically in today's world. Sadly and dramatically, our youth are clearly caught in this transition so characterized for them by broken value systems, violent attitudes, loneliness and a hunger for families that will not fail them. As with Fambrough, many of our youth feel stuck with no place to go. Yet they, along with Fambrough, are not to be pitied or judged but rather, understood. Fambrough's final words describe the hopelessness of the situation, "To your journey; to my journey," and again, "The King is dead, long live the King."

In the book version, the author, Michael Blake, makes it very clear that the death of Major Fambrough played an important part in Lieutenant Dunbar's severing all ties with the military. Fambrough's written orders were illegible. This, along with the death of the mule handler who took Dunbar to Fort Hays a hundred and fifty miles away, cut him off from all contact with the world he knew. To the military, it was as though he dropped off the face of the earth. He was truly on his own more than he knew.

FINDING THE LAND–
FINDING THE SOUL OF THE LAND

Leaving Fort Sedgewick, Dunbar is obsessed about one thing: to find the land as it has always been while it can still be found. Curiosity and wonder are his dominant attributes at this point. He asks, "Where are the buffalo?" "What about the Indians?" and, in a beautiful subtle moment, he extends his hands to the tall grass caressing it with a blessing that paves the way for his connection to Kicking Bird who, when we see him for the first time, is doing the same thing. Both love the land as well as horses. "*Washte*" (good), Kicking Bird says, patting Cisco admiringly. And as for Dunbar, it was only when he thought his horse was going to be stolen that he over-rode his fear and confronted the intruder. The horse is the symbol of creative liberated energy and becomes here for both Kicking Bird and Dunbar the expression of freedom and mobility. This is worth admiring and defending, for it was a reflection of the spirit of the place Dunbar was just beginning to experience. Symbolically, and especially in this story, the horse and the land go together.

Finding the land is finding the rhythm and harmony of the land. It is to accommodate oneself to a unity with it. Michael Blake describes Dunbar's life this way:

> There was no work and there was no play. Everything was one. It did not matter whether he was hauling water up from the stream or tying into a hearty dinner. Everything was the same, and he found it not at all boring. He thought of himself as a single current in a deep river. He was separate and he was whole, all at the same time. It was a wonderful feeling (p. 45).

The land can claim a person back quickly, and that is what is so frightening to many people. Yet, the land is our home and can, if we let it, awaken in us a familiarity that transcends boundary markers and property rights. It is our alpha and omega, the place of our origin and return. How could we not but feel a kinship with it that is as timeless as the earth itself. Yet the land and its soul lies buried beneath the conscious constructs of our times, beneath our cultural expectations of expand, produce and grow, a morality that is sickening people today. Cancer too is a growth, but a growth out of control that is no longer in harmony with the rest of the body but feeds on it and eventually destroys it. Our drivenness to dominate the land is a cancer in our time that has behind it a fear of the land itself. Normally we do not describe it this way let alone feel it, but not too far below the layer of our conscious awareness is a knowing that, if we let our guard down, the earth will take us back to Herself. How quickly our homes deteriorate, our lawns "go to weed," our nation's highways split apart when not cared for. How long would it take for the earth to claim back an average sized town of 20,000 if totally neglected. Would it take ten years, fifty years, or a century? In earth time, it is of little consequence, for, no matter how long it took, it would just simply happen. In short, the sense of our deteriorability has frightened us culturally into a political ethic that is prone to subjugate and depersonalize the earth as though it has no soul with which we can identity and relate. Is it any wonder then that so many people feel they are losing their soul or have lost it and visit the psychotherapist's office because they are anxious or depressed? Should we be surprised?

Fortunately, there is a growing awareness today among many that the land not only needs to be reclaimed but also ourselves in our relationship to it. This is what drove Dunbar into the unknown territory. His need to find the land was just another way of saying he needed to find himself in relationship to the land. He is that part of every one of us who has to not just get away but to reconnect with the land and the soul we will find there. Moving beyond our fear is critical to this discovery. When the Sioux gathered in council to decide what to do with this white man, it was Ten Bears, the elder leader, who said the needed statement, "When I see one man alone without fear in our country, I do not think he may be lost. I think he may have medicine." The aloneness has a lot to do with our own move toward an individuated life that dares to ask the vital questions and, if necessary, stand apart, to enter unknown territory with the "without fear"-ness attitude, that is, not letting the fear we have decide our actions.

Living at Fort Hays was Dunbar's threshold between the world he knew and could put in order and a world he increasingly became impatient to meet. He had reached the limits of his waiting and was tired of being anxious that he might be attacked. In one last military hurrah, he dressed himself in full uniform and rode out onto the prairie with little idea of what or whom he was to face. It is here that he meets the wounded and dying anima of two worlds, Stands with Fist.

Traditionally the idea of anima is that aspect of a man's

psyche that can be described as feminine. But anima is also soul imaged as woman, especially in a world so filled with masculine values. She is to be taken here not as the anima or feminine side of a man but as the anima or soulfulness of the spiritual journey of any person in our land. In fact, she could be taken as one image of the soul of our land. Like Lieutenant Dunbar and Major Fambrough, she too attempts suicide for the loss of her husband. She was now a widow. Remembering that this story is an account of the individuation journey of not only Lieutenant Dunbar but metaphorically of any single individual as well as our culture as a whole, then this encounter takes on greater meaning and depth. The word "individuation" means, at first glance, "not to be divided." And though this is true, its deeper meaning lies in the linguistic root of the word "divide" itself. It comes from two Greek words, *di,* meaning "apart," and *vidua,* meaning "widow/widower." Used together it would translate "apart as a widow." Thus adding the Greek word *in,* meaning "not," the word "individuation," at its core, means "not to be set apart as a widow/widower." So to find and tend her, to extend his compassion to her, was the critical turning point of the entire story. Everything would have come to a halt at this point if he had not attempted to reach out and help her. In doing so, unwittingly he was opening himself to the very world he had traveled so far to see. At the moment of his discovery, the ridiculousness of the persona of the world he wore and carried literally flew in his face. In two subtle moves it deteriorated in meaning. The first happens when the American flag flies in his face, interfering with his visual concern for the wounded woman. To this he simply and nearly inaudibly says, "Sonava bitch." The second is seen only when he is carrying Stands with Fist on his horse. He has ripped the American flag into bandages. It is a move not beyond pride and love for one's nation but beyond nationalism itself that pits people against one another and never sees or tends the wounded soul of the earth itself or ever gets to an understanding of how that might affect us.

On one level, Stands with Fist represents for the dominant culture the ability and unconscious desire to reunite with the sacredness of the land. For Native Americans specifically, she could carry the hope that indeed this is possible since, though she was white, they had found her, raised her and made her their own. She was one of them, had been brought up in their ways, and had their worldviews. If she is taken as but one anima soul image for Indian peoples themselves, then to be non-Indian is not nor should be seen as the problem, but rather to be inhuman, which indeed has been the experience of Indian peoples of the dominant white culture. Indian peoples historically have been more open to non-Indian people than the other way around, just as the land is far more ready to receive us than we the land.

The reason for this again lies in fear, but more directly fear of the unconscious itself, that is, of our inner world that has its own wilderness and uncharted territory. Here things are not laid out with such conscious intent but, in a no less real way, they have patterns and meanings of their own. Here are found our ancestral memories and the struggle and pain that brought consciousness into existence at all. It can feel all so dark and bloody and absolutely ridiculous and dangerous to regard. This seemingly unpredictable unconscious world appears to run counter to civilization as we know it and certainly is not conceived as the foundation or source of meaning and value for anything we would dare to call cultured at all. All this is projected onto the land itself and those peoples we consider close to the land as indigenous peoples–a projection that indicts us who have gotten so far from the land. In Africa, it is called "going black." On our continent it could be called "going red," a moving into savagery. The rejection of the earth and one's earth-ness results in a projection unto others of what we have failed for whatever reason to live responsibly in our own life. A blatant example of projection in the context of "going red" comes from a mid-nineteenth century Kansas City newspaper describing Native Americans:

> A set of miserable, dirty, lousy, blanketed, thieving, lying, sneaking, murdering, graceless, ruthless, gut-eating skunks as the Lord ever permitted to infect the earth, and whose immediate and final extermination all men should pray for.

Though these words sound ridiculous and extreme, it takes little imagination and a superficial reading of American history to know that the intent behind these words took on reality and continues in more subtle forms today.

On another but similar level, Stands with Fist is the anima or soul image of one who stands in the middle. She is of two cultures and knows the languages of both. This makes her the translator and vital to the process of reconciliation. In the same way, she is that side of our deeper self who lies wounded within, waiting to die or to be rescued. In so many ways, she is a reflection of the American collective soul needing to be discovered and tended. She is the force that can draw us back to ourselves as inhabitants of the earth as our home and bring us to celebrate rather than detest that our nativity is in the soil itself. Stands with Fist became Dunbar's entry ticket into Indian country as surely as paying attention to our own soul's woundedness individually or collectively is the entry place to discovering the riches of our own inner world.

The rest of the film is an unfolding of the process of the Indianization of Dunbar and the consequences this entailed. The viewer can see the gradual assimilation into Indian country. His hair gets longer, he gradually exchanges his clothing, he shaves, wears a feather and learns their language. He even eventually claimed his right to stand equally among them and be treated fairly when he insisted that his hat be returned to him–an incident that resulted in an exchange rather than a battle.

Entering this world, Dunbar became aware of just how lonely he really was in contrast to what he saw before him. Returning to Fort Hays, he built a large fire in the night and did his own dance around it, thrusting a crude spear in rhythmic motions that invited forth his own primal soul. It could have looked to an observer like a descent into that same kind of madness that killed Major Fambrough. Yet, here was a creative dance of madness or abandonment, the kind that strips away the exterior persona, giving us a glimpse of our more authentic self and the painful awareness of just how far we are from this. For Dunbar, it was the awareness of just how truly lonely he was: "Many times I've been alone, but until this afternoon, I've never felt completely lonely."

This dance of Dunbar's is similar to a dream of a thirty-eight year old male who defined his issue at this point of his life as seeking deeper spiritual meaning to his identity and the direction life wants him to go. He was a psychotherapist himself and quite psychologically reflective as well as committed to an active spiritual life. During the analysis he dreamed:

> I'm in a house and there are a variety of rooms. A man takes me into one of the rooms and leads me to the center. There is a rug in the center and there are feathers scattered on it. They appear to to have been stepped on. The man takes me to the center, holds my shoulders and looks me in the eyes and firmly says, "Now do what you need to do." He leaves the room and closes the door. I start to dance around the rug. It seems like a holy dance and something I must do. As I'm dancing, I notice that one of the walls of the room is covered with mirrors. I look at myself and then look away,

> not wanting to become self-conscious or to be performing. I want the dance to continue naturally.

This dreamer's dance is placed in the same context as Dunbar's though in a more modern version. The man in the dream, his initiator, takes him to his own center and tells him to do what he must do. Like Dunbar, he is left alone with reflections of himself, vis-à-vis the mirrors, needing to sort out what was "performing" or pretense in his life from that which was natural. Feathers, remnants of the winged-ones, symbols of the spirit, are scattered around and have been stepped on, which graphically conveys the spiritual life of many today. But it does not matter now. The dance must be performed because it is a holy dance integral to his fundamental self and one he must find out by himself.

Gradually Dunbar comes to a deeper awareness of himself. His relationship to the wolf, Two Socks, revealed a growing appreciation for that which was wild, untamed, and free. In the book, Michael Blake says of him:

> He was big and sturdy, but something about him gave Dunbar the impression he was past his prime. His coat was scruffy and the lieutenant thought he could see a jagged line along the muzzle, most likely an old scar. There was an alertness about him that signified age. He seemed to watch everything without moving a muscle. Wisdom was the word that came to the lieutenant's mind. Wisdom was the bonus of surviving many years, and the tawny old fellow with the watchful eyes had survived more than his share (p. 41).

Looking at Two Socks was like looking at himself, which he was only later to discover. A Native American friend told me he felt Two Socks represented the *Oyate,* a Lakota word for "the People," whether that be a nation or the entire world itself, though specifically, in this context, the reference is to the Indian people. It would seem then that *Oyate* would be that side of anyone that is rooted in evolutionary history, that is older than oneself and that carries the wisdom of the species. This side stares at us as certainly as Two Socks stared at Dunbar. The decision not to shoot him was another major turning point for his spiritual journey. Looking into the eyes of Two Socks, he was looking at something in himself.

Similarly, the male dreamer who dreamed of the dance also had this dream:

> Some of us from work are driving to a retreat house in the country. I'm sitting in the back seat with Martha and she is telling me about one of her friends. While I'm listening, I'm aware that a light rain has just fallen and nature is responding. Flowers are vibrant in bloom and all kinds of animals are out and playing. They are very visible just off the side of the road we are on. I see a beautiful light gray wolf in the field and I point it out to Martha. She gets angry at me and accuses me of not listening to her. I respond by telling her everything she said plus how beautiful the wolf was and that all the animals that are out are beautiful and we should be taking it all in.

The dream begins with leaving work and going to a retreat place in the country, that is, finding rest by returning to that which is natural. The opening sets the direction to look for the spiritual renewal and discoveries this man needed. Everything comes alive and intensifies with the rain, which literally is a dampening of the earth and symbolically is a moistening of the soul. The flowers and animals are off the road, that is, off the usual path the dreamer takes in life but not so far off they are inaccessible. An anima figure associated with his everyday world needs to be informed she is not being ignored but also challenged to appreciate the beauty of the wolf and of all the animals. The dream was trying to awaken the spiritual life of this man to the discovery and appreciation of the natural world within himself, its beauty and mystery. Like Two Socks, this wolf must not be ignored, for it too carries wisdom and insight from the older and more "uncivilized" region of our soul. Like the dreamer "we should be taking it all in."

Dunbar's relationship to Two Socks became so important that he was given a name honoring this friendship, Dances with Wolves. Of this he says, "I never knew who John Dunbar was, but, hearing my Sioux name being called over and over, I knew for the first time who I really was." This was affirmed later in a conversation with Kicking Bird who tells him, "I was just thinking that of all the trails in this life, there is one that matters more than all the others. It is the trail of a true human being. I think you are on this trail, and it is good to see." This scene marks this story as an individuation account finding deeper fulfillment and rootedness in the earth. But this is not without price.

He truly crosses over from the world he has known when he returns to Fort Hays. His horse, Cisco, gets killed, and he is beaten and put in chains to await a certain execution. Here it becomes clear to him that he is no longer one of them. They do not recognize him and he refuses to speak in their language. This is all summed up in Sergeant Bauer's words, "Gone Injun, haven't you?" to which he responds, "I have nothing more to say to you." The process of individuation can be costly. Instead of eliminating suffering, it can actually increase it by sensitizing the soul to what really matters in life and then trying to live in a world that discounts it.

This film is not without criticism. I have heard, "It does not deal with real life Native Americans on reservations today; it idealizes them," or "It is just another story of a white man and white woman falling in love." Whatever reply one would make for or against these criticisms, the story in total has been well received and even welcomed by both Indian and non-Indian peoples. Indian people were finally viewed as having heart and soul and a deep commitment to family and land, willing to live and die for a good cause and endowed with a great sense of humor. For some Indian people and for many more non-Indian people, this film is powerful because it touches our own struggle to find again a healing and creative relationship to our own soul, the land and the soul of this land. It is powerful also because it vividly portrays the attempt to find an authentic way of life over against a lifestyle that is killing most Americans. There is a sadness in this film too because it shows how relations could have been between Indian and non-Indian people throughout American history. Yet, it is also promising by intimating a way of reconciliation between, first, the dominant culture and Native American communities, and, second, between our dominant cultural ego orientations and the side of ourselves that waits longingly to live in harmony and relationship to the earth we are and the earth around us.

The Indian is that part of anyone that is at home in the earth, that speaks of relationships to the earth and that recognizes the sacredness of the ecosystem and the unity implied in the universe. The Indian is that side that is willing to play its part in an economy of stewardship based on sacred exchanges of giving and taking, that recognizes one Creator *(Wakan Tanka, Gitchie Manitu)* and that knows not color, race, class or disabilities. This one knows the earth as "Grandmother" and "Mother" and sees all things as living and in motion and endowed with the breath of the Creator. Such a view moves far beyond a Cartesian physics based on a compartmentalized view of the universe. This is the ultimate physics that places everything in relationship to everything else. One Native American man told a conference I attended that to be "Indian" was not so much a matter of genetics as it was a matter of spiritual attitude. It is also true then that to be "Indian" is to be a modern physicist who sees the entire universe as one package.

But as can easily be seen, this attitude is quite the opposite of what pervades our cultural milieu today. This has created an enormous cultural shadow of the existing constructs of our time that filter down to our individual shadow problems. I am using "shadow" here in the broadest sense to refer to that which has been left out of the field of consciousness whether on a cultural or individual level. It refers to what we do not know about ourselves and often gets projected onto others, whether it is the person next door or at the office or a group of people "different" from us. These projections can take the form of either looking down on someone in contempt, distrust or hatred or looking up in exaggerated idealizations. Both responses keep the "other" at bay and serve to keep us from facing the issues we see in those strange to us.

Though there is so much of ourselves we do not know and that will always stay in the unconscious, when it is time to grow and move along in our evolutionary journey, those issues that now need recognition and acceptance will come up with a force that cannot be stopped until consciousness and understanding are brought to them. This is what is in front of us today in Indian/non-Indian relationships specifically because we live on these North and South American continents. But generally it is a matter of indigenous/non-indigenous relationships or of seeing the earth as home or non-home or viewing matter as sacred or not sacred. These unresolved shadow issues are dividing the world today and will not just simply go away any more than my hatred for someone will go away until I come to grips not with the object of my hatred but with what I have not yet resolved in myself.

Most people seem spiritually weary today and many are growing more and more discontent with our culture. I see this as good because it signals a time to re-evaluate what we have lived and what has lived us. I see this as good because when people get weary and discontent enough, it usually leads to change. But in the meantime a great deal of suffering, burnout and cultural collapse will take place. Almost everyone nowadays has suffered the effects of being cut off from the land as a home and is paying the emotional and spiritual price for this. This includes Indian and non-Indian alike. For Indian people it has been through forced emigrations to territory not their own, through governmental and bureaucratic entanglements that destroy the right of self-determination, and through alcoholism and indifference to tribal history and land. For non-Indian people it is important to remember that we are still immigrants and children of immigrants collectively still in search of a land. We will truly not be home until we spiritually claim this land and let the land claim us as living and sacred. Today we hear a lot about anxiety, depression and ulcers. The three leading drugs in North America are used to treat these three problems. Perhaps behind these is a greater issue simply called despair, which is the result of our disconnection with the earth in a holy manner.

The suppressions of the feminine, the earth, indigenous peoples and our own indigenous side are all related to one destructive dynamic, the fear of the unconscious, the unknown, for all of these have carried projections of unresolved cultural issues. Old map makers used to mark unexplored areas or areas they knew nothing about with the words, "Here Be Monsters." We moderns are not so far from such an attitude as we relate to others we do not know or parts of ourselves that still remain unexplored. This is what Dunbar faced as he entered the unknown territory beyond his own civilization. This is what gets projected onto the earth as the primary carrier of the unknown and then onto anything or anyone that represents the earth like the feminine side of life or anything indigenous including our own inner world.

One can only ask then what the Christian doctrine of the incarnation means if matter has no spiritual value. We collectively recognize matter but not its sacredness. We recognize psychology but not necessarily *psyche,* soul. We recognize the female but not the value of the feminine. We recognize Native Americans as long as they do not make political noise or money. We recognize the earth as long as we can use it. For this, everyone pays a price–men, women, Native Americans, non-Indians, land, sky, water and all earth's children.

People are tired. When Dunbar was chained and stated that he had nothing more to say to them, that he speaks a different language, he might just as well have said, "I am tired of you defining life by management by objectives. I am tired of your system that shrinks the individual, that is proud of its killings, that exports its persona to other countries while forgetting its own soul. I am tired of you seducing my soul through corporate promises and advertising gimmicks. I am tired of you telling me what I crave to eat, wear, drink and drive or what my value should be. I am tired of waving little flags celebrating mass destruction and bastardizing what the American dream ought to really be about. I am tired of being drained at the end of a day instead of fulfilled. If only you would be interested enough to speak the soul's language, none of this would be necessary."

I do not believe such reactions are confined to just a certain class of people. It seems that blue and white collar workers alike are under the impact of the cultural disillusionment of success. This seems particularly evident in the professional scene where the rules are changing and the esprit de corps is breaking down. I remember years ago the renowned Jungian analyst, Dr. Marie-Louise von Franz, telling a group of us that in the middle ages, all groups of workers had a god or goddess governing them. Thus carpenters had Saturn, tailors had Hermes, dancers and artists had Venus, healers had Asclepius, statesmen and teachers had Apollo and Athena and so forth. They represented the spirit and enthusiasm (meaning the god or goddess in something) of the work that was also a vocation (meaning a calling) and not just labor. Today this is all in danger. People are leaving the professions. Teachers, police, medical doctors, clergy, psychologists and lawyers find themselves burned out, looking over their shoulders for lawsuits, working under demanding financial expectations for job performance and finding the joy of the work being replaced by emotional drain. Each of these as well as other professions could be taken apart and studied as to what each is going through, but what only needs to be stated here is that the god or goddess or the spirit of each of them has been sent into exile.

That which is fundamentally human in all of us, which has developed over millions of years of evolutionary history and which is just simply natural to all of us worldwide, is in danger today. The "natural," that which is of "nature," of our "nativity," our birth (as a species), is today defined by unnatural definitions. So what we are may best be stated by what we are not. It is not the way of things to make war, to kill our children, to separate ourselves from the earth, to grow old weak in spirit, to fear death, to abuse our children or children their parents, to despise our elders, to think of family as only mother, father, daughter and son, to think only others are artists and poets, to not dance, to not sing because you think you cannot, to not think of yourself as a spiritual being, to think you are so different from the rest of creation, to have even one orphan in the world, to despise our sexuality.

This list could go on, but it is the loss of just these kinds of basic ways of being human that makes us emotionally and physically ill. It is what robs the spiritual life of excitement and vitality and, in the worst situation, makes anyone want to blow his or her brains out as Major Fambrough did. Such losses create a profound alienation from ourselves at our most indigenous root. All have suffered and been victimized by these kinds of inhuman attitudes and beliefs. As the collective culture chased down Dances with Wolves and

Stands with Fist, so our own collective attitudes chase down, outdo, intimidate, silence and even destroy our own indigenous side, often in the name of progress or enlightenment or religious security.

In the closing scenes of the film, Dances with Wolves makes ready to leave the People to help secure their safety. He and Kicking Bird exchange pipes, a truly high and honorable recognition of their relationship in that the pipe is the most sacred instrument of prayer for many Indian people. He hears Wind in His Hair crying out from a bluff, "I am Wind in His Hair. Can you not see that I am your friend? Can you not see that you will always be my friend?" His connection to what he had been looking for has been sealed. Ten Bears tells him that the man the calvary is looking for no longer exists. In the book version, Ten Bears tells Dances with Wolves that there was no worry because when they came they would not find Lieutenant Dunbar but Dances with Wolves. Lieutenant Dunbar no longer existed; he was no longer one of them, so how could he be found? To the linear rational mind this sounds naive, but it holds a fundamental truth, namely, when you have found your soul and its relationship to the spirit of the land, you will not be recognized or understood by the standard of the world that would destroy these things. Though there will be conflict, you will be playing by a different set of rules, the rules of the soul.

These ending scenes recognize that Dunbar had finally gained all that was truly essential to his life. It stands in stark contrast to how the film began with him lying on a surgeon's table waiting to have his leg cut off. Now, at the end, there are just two people straddling two cultures with all the painful awareness and tension this brings but, at the same time, now searching for a new creative order.

This film is a prophetic story, a metaphor for our times, suggesting a day when lines will not be drawn between Indian and non-Indian, conservative and liberal, male and female, or east and west. These will soon be old battle demarcation zones that will make less and less sense as time goes by. The new lines will be drawn between those who love the earth and those who have forgotten Her, and between those who seek the sacred and those who have no regard for it. Most of all, these lines are to be drawn and discovered within ourselves and reconciled.

Chapter Four

A Personal Search: Seeking the Ancestor

...every individual problem is somehow connected with the problem of the age, so that practically every subjective difficulty has to be viewed from the standpoint of the human situation as a whole.

Carl G. Jung[13]

...a dream...will as a rule contain mythological motifs, combinations of ideas or images which can be found in the myths of one's own folk or in those of other races. The dream will then have a collective meaning, a meaning which is the common property of mankind.

Carl G. Jung[14]

There is a piece of land near my home along a river known as the Crayfish that eventually, via other tributaries, empties its waters into the Gulf of Mexico. This place is sixty acres of what is now called the Faville Prairie in Wisconsin, true virgin ground, ungrazed, unplowed, uninvaded by any foliage that was not meant to be there. It was once part of twenty-five hundred acres that is now mostly farmland. In the Faville section, each plant has found its niche in the swells and swales of the topography. Each has ecologically tuned itself to the other. This last remaining section of land was saved in the eleventh hour by a local farmer who persuaded a Milwaukee couple to buy it a day or two before cows were to be let loose on it for grazing. They in turn gave it to the University of Wisconsin Arboretum which has been managing the prairie ever since.

Aldo Leopold was a part of the initial study and caretaking of this last remaining piece of virgin land near my home.

Late one afternoon, my wife and I and several of our friends walked this land with our guide, and here we found land as it always was, land undisturbed by human intention, like the last bit of color on a fading flower. It was a profound experience awakening something fresh, primal and uncontaminated. Near the end of our walk we decided to sit or lie on the ground in silence and allow the land to speak. And that it did. It was then that my wife had a distinct vision as she was staring at a large tree nearby. As she closed her eyes, she first saw that she was the tree and then, again, saw it separate from her. It was large, and birds made their nests in it and fed there. She saw herself standing in the center of the tree where the many branches forked out, and she thought, "What a great place to make a tree house or platform" (her nest). As she thought this she saw a light-blue light conveying energy shoot up from the trunk. She realized this blue light came from deep in the earth and used the tree as its conduit. This is a vision of living matter, of the Spirit in Nature or of matter ensouled.

I was sad when we left Faville later that evening. And I became sadder when we turned onto the highway leading back to our small community with its lights and traffic and concrete. I felt sad for the land, sad for the many peoples of this land and sad for the little piece of virgin soil that reminded me of the original home from which we came and of which we are still a part, the earth. I was as sad as the child who had just seen its parent after a long absence and just as quickly lost that parent when he or she left.

What we experienced that evening and what my wife saw is a brief metaphor for what many people are suffering in our times. Increasingly today people share with me in the consultation room their growing sense of soullessness and pointlessness in their jobs and lives. This is expressed frequently in rage and sadness over their disconnection from the earth and what is happening to it. At the same time and in an inverse manner, it is as though the more our earth home goes into decline, the more small, silent and unnamed groups of people are gathering to intervene through understanding and action.

The notion of matter containing soul is certainly contrary to the western understanding of matter being soulless and dead. Yet imagine it having a soul of its own as certainly as we humans do. Imagine matter having or being soul in the sense of containing something ancient, vital, moist, growing and intentional–in other words, full of meaning and design. The earth, then, would be something we would have to be in relationship with, much as we would with a relative or friend. It would be something we could not avoid or misuse without consequences. It would mean we would have to recognize the interdependency of all things and acknowledge that whatever is done to one aspect of earth affects all of it.

For now, let us imagine the earth being ensouled and, as metaphor, carrying its own image of itself in the form of our own ancient original indigenous side. For those of us on the American soil, it takes the form of the Native American who has been the carrier of important projections for non-Indian peoples. These projections evoke those fundamental earth qualities inherent in all of us along with a sense of intimacy and familiarity with the earth. These projections have also resulted in both idealization and near annihilation. That which we so desperately want to reconnect with is also that which terrorizes us, namely, the Indigenous One and the indigenous territory within ourselves. In North American political history, "Indian Country" was that area of our continent needing to be "settled" and "civilized." Indian Country was a nuisance, a problem and dangerous. This term was even still used during the Vietnam conflict to refer to the jungle area where one could easily get killed.

Consider now, however, Indian Country from another perspective, not as a place to survive and conquer but as a place to enter for renewal. In psychological terms, going into Indian Country would then be meant to describe the journey into our deepest self which includes by reference our earth-rooted indigenous ground. It would not be necessary for us to go to a literal reservation but to that "reserve" within ourselves where the Indigenous One has been contained, suppressed and all but forgotten. Any movement into Indian Country as such is a turning toward home and a recognition there of our most essential and deepest self. It is to raise up before ourselves the earth as it is and the earth that we are. If we talk then about the Indigenous One which, as I am saying, on the American continent is carried by the American Indian, we must talk about matter as living and, if we talk about matter as living, we must talk about the Indigenous One. This is true simply because the Indigenous One, as living psychic reality, is so only because the earth itself is endowed with life. I contend that this relationship, though basic, is utterly foreign to the western way of thinking and living.

My own experiences are similiar to those of many others who have been raised and educated in the western tradition. This tradition has been rich and generous in shaping who I am and how I look at life both within myself and around me. But along the way, I grew increasingly aware that something was missing. Two things stand out in the last twenty-five years that helped me eventually to understand that something was not right. I became deeply involved, first, with the work of Dr. Carl Jung, and, second, with the workings of Native American spirituality. Jung, as a westerner, provided the tools that opened up the doors to the vast treasures of the inner world and gave value to it. He demonstrated that the inner world is ancient and intentional and is as internally deep as the stars are externally. This internal archetypal world carries life and nourishment and is the mother of all civilization. I had always felt this way but had never been taught it in all my previous experiences. It was as if my soul said "Yes, there it is—finally voiced."

Jung had a deep regard for the earth, which anyone who knows his story or writings can quickly surmise. He also had a deep regard for the American soil and for the aboriginal peoples of this earth, believing that the non-Indian immigrant to this land was deeply affected by the soul of these original peoples. He described what was called an Indianization process that happened to all non-Indian immigrants in a mostly unconscious way but which came to distinguish them from their homes of origin. It is as though the soul of the American soil and its first peoples rises up and influences and even wants to adopt the outsider. In our own land it has been seen in the conqueror taking on the attributes of the conquered.

All of this, however, remains still in the academic realm. I am sure Jung would agree that none of this would make any personal sense unless we look for this process within ourselves. Individually we need to discover how this land has personally affected us as well as the culture that we not only live in but which lives in us. In my own case, the myth (story) of the Indigenous One in the form of the American Indian stayed as psyche's metaphor creating a tension between its worldview and the world I had known. At the same time, it became the symbol for healing the split between these two worlds most of us feel. It needs to be said that the reason is not that I had no regard for the land. To the contrary, I, as many people do, had a very close connection to the earth all my life. But my awareness really was not consciously that of earth as home or mother or living matter. Over recent years, it was as though my inner Self took me by the nape of the neck and said, "Okay, so you love the earth. Let's just see how far and deep you are willing to go." What in fact happened over the years was a constant flow of dreams involving Native American issues that spoke directly to my own spiritual journey and, I believe, to the spiritual crisis of our culture. Though the dreams I will present here are mine, they could just as well, with some variations, be the dreams that any of us could have insofar as we all live on this continent and feel its pain. Indeed it is my hope that the reader will take these dreams with this collective perspective in mind. It is not my intent to indulge myself but rather to amplify through these dreams what I believe to be major concerns for all of us today, both non-Indian and Indian alike.

About fifteen years ago, I had an astounding dream that I will never forget and which acts as a fitting place to begin:

> I was in a building that gave the appearance of being a church with vaulted ceilings. It was a holy precinct. I remember looking at an ancient Bible written in English script. I could read parts of it. It was beautifully done. I had the Bible open and was unable to read the title of the section before me. The script was too difficult. Now a man who is like a priest or holy man—my spiritual mentor or guide, I sense—tells me to go behind an altar upon which stood an intricate carving. He said, "Go behind it and you will see something that will bring you to your knees." I knew he had been through something significant. I had some doubt, however, about anything bringing me to my knees. Nevertheless, I went behind it and looked. First, I looked off into the distance on the inner walls of the church and saw various carvings intricately done. I saw one on a corner area that was gargoylish looking. I thought, "Maybe he is referring to that—to the principle of evil." But it did not seem to be this. Then I looked again at the carving before me from behind the altar. Meanwhile, the man was just sitting, knowing what would happen. The far right of the carving was a large horseshoe-shaped bone that had a name I cannot remember. It was the beginning. Out of this cornucopia-like bone carving and con-

> tinuing from it was a series of all kinds and manners of prehistoric animals that moved to the left. Aside from a large dinosaur that dominated the middle of the carving, there were snakes, lizards, a white mammoth with long legs and other long extinct creatures. To the extreme left of the carving and ending it was a small delicate carving of a human being. Upon seeing this, I broke into instant and uncontrollable weeping—a weeping founded in having had a holy mystery revealed to me—of having entered upon a profound and basic insight. I wept and wept and went out from behind the altar, sat down and wept some more. The man just sat there knowing what I had gone through.

Such a dream, I thought! What indeed can bring the twentieth century person to his or her knees? In the dream, I thought it had something to do with the principle of evil. But evil does not seem to bring anyone to his or her knees in our times. We might be shocked or horrified by it but not brought to our knees. It was the request to go behind the altar, that is, to look at the place of sacrifice from the unorthodox or not usually seen or accepted point of viewing, where the revelation would be made. Indeed it was the realization that we humans are intimately connected to all of life now and with all that has gone before us. This connection has been a bloody evolutionary process of birth, death and mostly sacrifice. The earth itself must now be seen as the altar upon which the great transformations and discoveries are made. It is also the one symbol that can unite us all since we are all of it and on it. It was the delicate and humble size of the human being carved there that broke me into weeping, knowing now its profound relationship to all that had preceded it. Acknowledging the profound connection to this indigenous ancestor pushes the notion of "Honor thy father and mother" to the furthest limit. This is the Indigenous One within us. It is a dream of earth and origins and of our most fundamental and delicate connection to all things.

This ancient being has been subdued and forgotten by the western way of life—a way of life that has uprooted itself from the earth and the earth we are. It has made harsh demands on the fundamental ways of the soul: how we worship, how we play, how we structure family, how we politic, how we run our economy, or how we imagine the future unto the seventh generation. This notion of the seventh generation comes from parts of the Native American world that believes that any important decision must be made with the question always in mind: How will it affect the seventh generation from now? To reclaim then the earth as a living soulful body and, at the same time, to redeem the inner Indigenous One are simultaneous tasks for each of us and for our culture as a whole. The loss of our connection to the earth and of our own fundamental nature has caused untold sadness that has come off as rage, apathy, and despair. Will the human community come to see itself as part of the "swells and swales" of the ecological balance determining life on this planet?

This question goes to the heart of the matter. Either we all will see our indigenous side and our indigenous responsibility to care for the earth, or the earth, with all its peoples, will die. The human community is to further recognize that there is no spiritual life of any worth that is disconnected from our fundamental self and the soil as our mother and origin. Unless this awareness is held as basic to our way of life, there will be no earth or soul to pass on to our children seven generations from now.

Today it is common for enlightened technologized peoples to talk about the indigenous peoples throughout the world as being the keepers of the land not only today but for thousands of years. What we must now realize, however, is that we also of the technologized world are indigenous peoples at some forgotten place within ourselves and, at one time, had a living indigenous past with a sense of intimately belonging to the earth. Indigenous really refers to an attitude and a way of life that respects the unity and relationship of all things on the earth.

For us to forget such roots can result in sentimentalizing the remaining six hundred million indigenous peoples of the world. It promotes an us/them division that keeps projections of our own forgotten ancestral life actively placed on "them." At the same time, it is true we have much to learn from such known keepers of the land about what we have long forgotten.

Over the years I have struggled to work on my own projections onto the Indigenous One, specifically the American Indian. Rather, it would be more accurate to say such projections have struggled with me in the forms of dreams, synchronistic events and deeply meaningful experiences. One of many dreams occurred years ago and turned the focus on my own role in this matter:

> I saw a fine pair of beaded moccasins that were just like the ones I had been looking for. They were light-colored, of a blue-tan tone. I picked them up and saw the price was $40. I knew I already had twenty dollars on me. Money was not the issue though. I needed to see what size they were but could not find the marking for the size. If anything, I was not concerned for the price but I feared they were too large for me (December 1982).

This dream came in the wake of having been invited to be the only non-Indian participant in a conference on Native American Spirituality presented by Native peoples for non-Indians. I had been asked not just because of my interest in Indian matters, but because of my training in Jungian work with its concern for dreams, symbols and cross-cultural parallels. As honored as I was, I was mostly nervous and not sure at all of what I had to offer. I saw the dream even at that time as not only related to my feelings about the conference but also questioning just how matters would evolve in the years to come.

This dream brought before me the issue of my taking on another kind of spirituality associated with Indian peoples. The fine pair of beaded moccasins was the symbol for this. I associated light-blue-tan as a spiritual color. To walk in these shoes myself would be the challenge. I personally had to purchase this position with an invested value I already partially had (twenty dollars). That they cost forty dollars does suggest that any further investment on my part in such a spiritual system would bring with it a greater sense of wholeness. (Four and any combination of four often, as symbol, carry the meaning of wholeness.) Yet the heart of the dream is not even this investment or my willingness to make it, but whether such an indigenous earth-connected spiritual position is too big for me to walk in. Or, in a reverse manner, are the spiritual feet I stand on too small?

My dream of many years ago is a dream any one of us could have that would challenge us toward a deepening connection of our western spiritual life form with the earth under us. In fact if this dream were taken as a collective dream, it could raise the question of not only whether we recognize the earth as a beautiful commodity, something we might even be able and willing to invest in, but also as holding a unique spiritual value long forgotten but ready to be assumed or worn as a way of life as a people. It also suggests that this spiritual attitude might not fit us, that is, might even be bigger than the traditional western way of looking at life.

It was not long after this dream that I had my first experience of what has come to be known as a "vision quest." Through a succession of names, places, and events, I found myself in the summer of 1984 on the Rosebud Sioux Reservation in South Dakota being taken to a lonely site and left without food or water. How did I get here? Curiosity and naiveness truly pave the way for unusual events. It was here that I became aware of a sense of my mortality. At the end of the second day, and as evening drew near, I thought that I could die here this night and no one would know it. How easily life can come and go. It was a deepening experience that brought more insights to me, my western tradition, the earth and the culture I live in. On my return home, my family and I stopped for the night at a campsite near the freeway. I remember sitting on a picnic table listening to the traffic pass a short distance away and feeling a chill go up my spine–a chill of recognition of being caught in the middle. I was not a part of the Indian community that so graciously held me, but I also did not feel any longer that I was a part of the community I was going back to. The chill also had to do with wondering if I could maintain the kind of spiritual integrity I had gained on that "vision experience" when I returned to the usual hectic cultural pace we all live in.

Being "caught in the middle" does not seem to be unique to me. Many people are no longer sure of where to find spiritual integrity in our times. Many in the Judeo-Christian world are sitting on the edges of their religion and no longer able to go to or find meaning in their churches or synagogues but also are not able to give up their faith views either. It just does not make sense anymore; what looks like apathy on the surface is underneath really sadness and frustration over having a faith with no place to go. It is as though the wine (the faith) is rich but the wineskins (the institutions) are old and leaking. How then do we exist if not often in denial of the problem and repression of the fundamental needs of the soul through hyperactive living?

My experience of sitting on the picnic table, stuck in the middle, I now see is as the suffering of most people in our times. Most of us, when we break through the persona of our culture and the lifestyles that influence us, find that we are foreigners in our own land. The Judeo-Christian spiritual tradition via Europe has a hard time claiming the soul of this land. In fact, it is against this European tradition to even conceive of the land as having soul. From the beginning, the two views of seeing the land as either dead or as having a soul, a living entity, were the cause of the great worldview division between European and Indian cultures. This division formed a corresponding split within the western psyche of non-Indian peoples that paralleled the tragic historical split between European and Indian people along with the ways of life they represent. The fantasy of my death on the second night of my quest is the very issue the western worldview wants to avoid. Earth and its matter are the enemy carrying that dreaded pronouncement, "Ashes to ashes, dust to dust." Earth and death are the enemies we have been told about by the western Christian paradigm, thus deepening the internal split that would accept the fullness of life and death as part of the same process and matter as the stuff of our soul's incarnation.

An example of this split between Indian and non-Indian views of spirituality is seen in a dream I had within a year after this vision quest experience:

> I dreamed I was standing in the entryway of a church where it connected with a new addition that had just been built. I had been wearing deer antlers on my head, though now I did not have them on. I was without a shirt and was wrapped in a vision-questing blanket. The pastor of the church, in full clerical garb, came to me and said he was angry and that I knew why. He said he did not need to say anything else. I said, "Yes I know." He responded that he wanted a change right away. He was referring to the issue of my dressing more appropriately. As I emerged from sleep, a last dream thought came to me: "He is not my boss, and I must indeed tell him that."

I was familiar with this church and with this particular

pastor. He was a good man, someone I respected and had a high regard for. There had just been a new addition built and, in the dream, I actually was standing in the place that joined the old and new together. These associations show the subtleties not only of the dream but also of the problem it addresses. Aside from what this dream says about my own struggle, it points to a dilemma faced by much of our culture today. Two spiritual points of view faced off against each other in this dream. Although not in any crude or obvious manner, western North American religion at its best and in full Christian clerical garb found little room in its sacred arena for a spirituality that would dress or present itself with an indigenous point of view. Nor could it even imagine the sacredness of such a presence symbolized by the questing blanket and the deer antlers which really are a crown given by the earth itself. Such a one just does not belong in the existing mind-set of western religion. It is just much too wild, much too earthly, much too illogical. It is also less linear in thinking, more unified in its view of cosmos, and thus less concerned with parochial divisions. This one is not into power but concerned with the relationships of all things. It does not wish to dominate the earth but intimately belongs to it. It does not wish to eliminate western religion but to be included in it. In short the division does not need to be but is the result of a fearful near-paranoid imagination of an over-rationalized age. It cannot be the ruling principle (the boss); the issue needs to be addressed, and can be.

Christendom in the western world has not in practice claimed the earth as truly sacred. A view of the doctrine of the incarnation as referred to in Chapter Two holds that matter can be a carrier for the sacred spirit of life. Yet it is a doctrine that has for the most part been deferred to the person of Jesus of Nazareth at one point in history and certainly not to all aspects of creation. It is hardly seen in its cosmic sense, because it has been so literalized. In its broadest context, it challenges our understanding that life is in all things and, because of this, extends our conception of responsibility and compassion accordingly.

The western Christian paradigm is ultimately one of compassion for the underprivileged, the poor, sick, hungry and homeless, and all who suffer. But filtered through political misuse of power, both the state and the church, with sword or dogma, turn compassion to judgmentalism, indifference and brutality. The message of compassion and the medium of this message have a tragic history. Today the western religious tradition is faced with its own vital need to re-evaluate its practice and language that will better reflect what I believe it really wants to stand for. Many within this tradition have worked hard to maintain the integrity of this message and to present themselves in a way that is open and caring to the world around them. But the issue is not those people; it is the system behind them. Such caring ones often themselves become the victims of the system they represent as they attempt to minister lovingly. This condition takes on ironic sadness in that the church holds the key to its own recovery in the very message it purports to proclaim. Compassion now, however, must not be defined only as general relief or caring for another person or people but as a full embracing of and identification with the earth itself. It is to see the earth now as the one that suffers and is in need of care. It is to stretch our understanding of compassion to include all aspects of the earth. For example, imagine having compassion for the soil or water or air or trees or animals or the general landscape. How would this change our attitudes and ethical sensitivities in our everyday use of these things? Such a question is on the cutting edge of needed change for all those who belong to or are affected by the western Christian tradition.

The second night of the first time I vision quested I had a dream that addressed these very issues:

> I was in a church building. A pastor I knew was in his study saying he had persuaded the church council to get him an updated dictionary saying, "How do they expect me to write letters and communicate unless they did?" I went to get some water from a drinking fountain. It was not cold. I asked for ice and was directed to a refrigerator. Inside I saw beer and knew it was just not right to use that to refresh myself. Then I saw ice–lots of it. I thought it a good idea to always keep ice water in the refrigerator in the church.

There are two important aspects to this dream. The first is the need for an updated dictionary. The pastor who requested it is the same man I previously said I highly respected. He is like a metaphor for my own struggle and for the church as a whole to redefine its language in a way that can be understood in today's world with today's problems, keeping in mind the earth as one body of which we are all a part.

The second aspect of the dream had to do with finding refreshing water. The church has always made much of water as a symbol for life and renewal. It is used in baptism and the ritual of washing of the feet as a sign of servanthood. The dream says the water is there in the church but it is not refreshing. It should be remembered that I was without water for two and a half days on this vision quest. By the time of this dream, water had become a literal symbol of life for me. Its absence had become a part of the immediate sense of my own mortality. Without it I could die. When a person is at such levels of dehydration, the idea of cool refreshing water takes on agonizing proportions and lays the ground for such a dream where the soul can declare its parallel need. The water of the spiritual tradition of the west does not stir the soul the way it once did. As a result then, sometimes a substitute is symbolically used as represented in the beer which I knew would not be appropriate. There is no substitute for the living water of life itself. No matter how much our culture deludes itself into thinking that this or that way of living is the real thing, if it is not reflecting the life force that is in all creation, it is like an intoxicant that dulls our awareness of what our soul really needs. The western Christian tradition is not without water; it just needs to make it more refreshing and drinkable to itself and the world of which it is a part.

This is an age of seeking new meanings to the metaphors that govern our lives. Words have different definitions, given their context and those using them. In addition, certain words can come to represent things they were never meant to convey, words like salvation, forgiveness, good and evil, truth, honor or love itself. Words and language can become, like the unrefreshing water of my dream, unable to move the soul because they do not themselves carry soul any longer. They have come to mean different things often reshaped by the politics of the time. The word "democracy," for example, meant one thing in the nineteenth century, another thing in the twentieth, and hopefully still another in the twenty-first. In each of these times, it did not mean the same thing to everybody. For example it meant one way of life for white people and another for black people. Because of this, the need is always there to struggle to give ever new meanings to such a word. Likewise the language of the cultural religious structures that have influenced us for the last two millennia are in need of constant redefining. It is as though a word ought to grow or take on flesh, that is, deepen its incarnational meaning of the soul it carries in its ancient core root. As the dream says, an updated dictionary is needed. Two months later in another dream, the same point was made again.

> I needed to get a Random House Dictionary for somebody. It seems it was for the church. I thought of giving the one I

had or getting one for that person because I could get it cheaper than someone else.

In the process of redefining words or rewriting history or recognizing the ancient core roots within us that give us depth, the use of the term "Indigenous One" is a way of describing the image that must be kept before us. Today there are many attempts to reconnect with our indigenous nature via the Native American. I am glad for this awakening but am also concerned for the caution needed. Years ago, a Makah Indian woman casually and caringly said to me, "Take your time, Fred, take your time." As the years have gone by, I have come to appreciate her wise words. In our attempts to find the earth again as our home, the Indian can easily become the "object" of imitations and idealizations. It is easy to do this because of our hunger. The result can be superficial dabbling leading to inflationary moments. The New Age-ism of our time can make a financial killing from our desperate need to reconnect with the earth and our own aboriginal side. At the same time, I am sympathetically aware we must begin somewhere. It is not "Do we?" or "Don't we?" but what attitude we shall assume as we proceed. If we go into "Indian Country" spiritually speaking, let us go in with our shoes off, that is, let us go in gently and respectfully lest we violate something or someone even though we did not intend to do so. Usually for the westerner this means to silence for a while our need for explanations and logical understandings. It means to put a hold on our Europeanized way of explaining reality and be open instead to the unusual, sometimes even the bizarre, and certainly the synchronistic event.

It is a question just how close we are to "Indian Country" or the aboriginal world we long ago left behind. I have come to believe this line between the two worlds is really quite thin. On the surface, we daily live a high-tech fast-paced life that makes it easy to forget our relationship to the earth and the earth as an ecosystem that has held and nurtured us from the beginning. We can be so detached that we talk about nature as some "place" or "event" we experience for a while, usually on vacation, and which we must "leave" in order to "get back to reality." Actually, it is the other way around. Nature, whether it is in the city or in the countryside, is the fundamental reality we are a part of. It is constantly with us, even if only in our unconscious world. Because our five hundred year history has created an unfortunate division between these two worlds, to move from one to the other can create spiritual bends. I have seen this happen going on wilderness canoe trips. The ego quickly loses its grip on the familiar and descends to other truths and realities related to the broad ecosystem from which we have been shielded. Here there is little room for arrogance or cocksuredness but a great deal for respect and awareness that one is a part of the greater scheme of things. Here one does not talk about the elements but rather experiences them intimately. And if one looks with just a little imagination, he or she can feel that connection with all things having their origin in a common cosmic history.

In my own attempts to cross this thin line into "Indian Country," I have made mistakes in the form of inflation, dabbling, imitating or idealizing. Yet to proceed at all requires mistakes as well as the admission of them. They become our teachers and marking points for the next discovery. Mistakes do not violate the soul so much as their denial or refusal to be challenged.

There were experiences and dreams that guided me along the way. In 1987, I went on my fourth vision quest experience. Late in the evening of the first night and quite alone, I had a liminal dream of someone being in my vision quest site. The details of this dream are not appropriate to talk about here, but I related them to what I experienced the next morning at dawn. When I was taken to my vision site the previous day, the medicine man and his helpers had surrounded my site with a long string containing six hundred tobacco tie offerings to the spirits. My site was "sealed" with this unbroken string of prayer ties. When I awakened on this particular day, this string of tobacco ties was broken in multiple places of varying lengths. There was no known explanation. It had never happened before. I was scared and tried in every western manner of thinking to give logic to this phenomenon. I have come to accept the unexplainability of that moment which now serves as a strong reminder and teacher that sometimes all we are required or even able to do is to hold these things in our hearts and wait.

Another event that acted as a warning and also as a turning point took place a year later. During a visit of a Lakota friend who was a well-respected teacher, a sweat lodge experience had been arranged. Several people came to be a part of this and the enthusiasm was high. I had spent a great deal of time and energy to prepare this event for the people and my friend. Looking back, I question if I was not perhaps even a bit manic in my attempt to make sure everything went well. When everyone was in the lodge and just before I was to enter, I reached up to pull the door coverings down. As I did this, I stepped back and heard a snap under my foot. I had broken the stem on my sacred pipe that was to be used during this ceremony. During the ceremony, I mentioned what had happened and said I would think about what this would mean. It was actually the second time it had been broken in one week. Soon after, my Lakota friend kindly but honestly said he thought I should bury my pipe and give it back to the spirits–in short, let it go. I was crushed. I then went to get a second pipe of another friend of mine, which happened to be on the altar mound outside the door, to use in the ceremony and realized I had broken his also. He calmly said he would bury his as well.

When I was advised to bury my pipe, I felt as though something had died in me. I mark this as an important transition event because it made me even more aware that the sacred pipe and all it represented was indeed real to me in the deepest way. It was integral to me and, because so, I need not ever get defensive in the face of criticism given by Indian or non-Indian for being in relationship to it. At the same time, I felt a renewed warning to take my time and watch how I place my feet both literally and figuratively.

Almost three years later I had a dream that could be called "The Guru Must Die." The guru in this case was a medicine man of great respect who had opened himself to me and had guided me on four vision quests, and, by this time, three Sun Dances. I thought well of him and he of me, but the dream addresses the issue of the "guru medicine man phenomenon" and gives a direction. I will call him Alex.

> Alex and I and some others were down by a river. I was catching and pointing out turtles. Alex died and I felt responsible. I was scared to tell the Indians for fear they would kill me. I went back to where they were. There were some very distinct Indian looking people there. Finally I got the courage and said I had some bad news, that Alex had died. There was no hostile reaction. Then I said it may also be good because now we would all have to take responsibility for our spiritual lives and not put it on Alex. An Indian said the same thing or simply agreed.

Without going into all the nuances of the dream, the heart of it lies in the personal need "to take responsibility for our spiritual lives." What truer words can be said in an age that does not encourage this. Yet the Indian or Indigenous One within ourselves knows this to be true and fundamental for the integrity of the spiritual life. No one can truly answer for you but you yourself. This is still strongly adhered to by traditional Native peoples today. For non-Indian peoples who are sensitive to the issues of spirituality, there may be a craving to reconnect to what Indian people represent. The risk of fixating on a guru is high and understandable. Unless it is faced, however, it becomes a problem for all concerned.

Everyone plays his or her part in the whole and is equally required to take responsibility for his or her own spiritual life. In keeping with this was a dream I had shortly after the previous one:

> The Sun Dancers had the task of keeping an airborne object like a kite in the air. This object was called *Canku Wakan,* that is, Sacred Road.

The Sun Dance is the supreme ceremony of the Plains Indians carrying in its liturgical drama the struggle and hope of all of the people and all creation for renewal. Clearly the dream is saying it is the task of each individual to struggle to keep such a spiritual life or "Sacred Road" aloft, that is, conscious. It is a task involving alertness, intent, collective responsibility and attention to the Sacred.

In a more western fashion this task is often undertaken in a psychotherapeutic or analytical container. Keeping the "Sacred Road aloft" is often expressed in the consulting room as "I am not sure where my life is going anymore" or "I feel depressed" or even "My kids are driving me nuts" or "I do not feel close to my partner anymore," etc. Not far below our conscious concerns are the deeper matters of just what our lives are ultimately connected to anyway. When what we want is lost or gained, we are still left with our own inner sacred path and our commitment and courage to follow it or not. It seems today that with the decline of traditional religious structures, an increasing number of people are seeking more meaningful connections to the "religious life." The therapist's office has become the sanctuary for this search. Sadly, clients are often more aware of this than the therapists themselves. Carl Jung put it this way:

"Everything to do with religion, everything it is and asserts, touches the human soul so closely that psychology least of all can afford to overlook it."[15] I returned to my own analytic sanctuary in a dream a year after the "guru" dream:

> I was with my analyst who now had a little gray goatee under his mouth. I had my sacred pipe and he had two of them. A stem was loose on one of them, perhaps both, but it did not seem to matter. I held one of them. His pipe was able to "clean" mine. Then his wife came and said, "I'm going to dance in the Sun Dance."

My analyst had been dead now for many years. He was a brilliant man with unusual generosity and love for the peasant lifestyle, the land and the simple life. To this day, I hold a deep respect and regard for him. It is fitting then that my dream returns me to what he represents as my own inner analytic perspective or soul's reflection on itself. He often spoke to me of "twoness" as the emphasizing of something important. It is now the pipes that connect us or, more accurately, those same aspects within myself. That my pipe was able to be cleaned by connecting it to his has something to do with keeping connection with the reflective analytic process. Not to do this can contaminate the sacred path with needless fantasies, literalizing, inflation, distorted ideations and so forth. The dream also shows in its own way that the European and Native perspectives of life need not be at cross-purposes. Finally, that his wife is now going to the Sun Dance serves to emphasize that this reflective analytic process and the anima behind it can serve well the indigenous spiritual core of the soul in a truly cooperative and celebrational way.

The earth is our home, a simple but forgotten or, at best, sentimentalized fact. Moving into ever deeper ecological awareness moves us into the mystery of matter itself and our intimate connection with it. Whether expressed through the science of the new physics or by western and native theological views, the universe is one place, seamless, interconnected and intentional. That which is from the beginning in us, that shares a lineage to the moment of the Big Bang, the truly Human Being (literally: "existing of soil"), knows this. Because of the western split-off from this understanding, the "Ancient One" in us has become quite autonomous, acting often as an inner critic, guide, benefactor, or waler for what is lost, or, all too frequently, just as a quiet waiting one. To raise to consciousness this indigenous nature of ours requires commitment, care, and certain consequences. The reason for this is that the more we become aware of our basic nature, the more we will be equally aware of all that which keeps us from it by the way most of our lives are conditioned in our times.

The following three dreams are personal examples of the subtle warnings given by the inner Native One. These are concerns anyone spiritually entering Indian Country must be mindful of:

> I dreamed that a powerful medicine man whom I know was approving what we were doing (that is, how we were running sweat lodge ceremonies). There was something here about foxes. Someone said he was due to go to prison for a while. I had heard he had gotten into trouble. It was as if he was already in prison.

Though the blessing of being on the right track is there, so is the consequence. The very one who knows the authentic or right way is also the one imprisoned. And this is the point most world religions make, namely, that the more the spiritual life is lived with integrity within oneself, the more one will experience the imprisoning imposed by the world that has little tolerance for it.

The second dream involves a young man who is emerging as a powerful teacher and leader to the Lakota people. He is also a man I am close to and for whom I have deep respect. I will call him Miles:

> I was talking with Miles and asking him about the kind of hide to use for a drum. He said deer hide was not good because it was too thin. I asked about cow hide, to which he emphatically responded, "No!" I think he went on to suggest something like elk hide.

The drum is the definitive musical instrument for the Native American. It is the heartbeat of the earth and creates a sound as old as the human race. At the same time, the drum lives in each of us as the beating of our own heart or in the involuntary movement of the body I have seen so often at ceremonial or powwow dances. It is as though the inner drum just needs an invitation from the outer literal drum to set itself in motion through body and soul. The dream takes on an intensity around the possibility of using cow hide and the response of "no!" Elk hide is preferred. I take this to mean that we cannot set or define the rhythm of the indigenous world with the standard of the western world. We must rather meet it on its own terms. It is so difficult not to interpret another culture or way of life using the premises with which we have been raised. This is true not only for non-Indian people but for Indian people as well. Misinterpretations have gone both ways. Elk hide or cow hide—both are ways of covering a drum, both will make a sound, but individually they symbolize two different ways of life. At this point, elk hide is now required, that is, something more indigenous must be recognized and heard for the welfare and heartbeat of this continent.

The third dream shows how demanding dreams can be. When we think we are on the right track and are confident that we have done our psychological homework, a dream may come and speak as though we have hardly begun. Such dreams serve to keep us mindful if not indeed humble. The man in the dream, whom I will call Joe, is also a respected leader and prominent teacher:

> I was with Joe who said that people who were just coming to rituals without commitment should not come. It was for third world people, i.e., Indians, Hispanics, blacks, etc.–in other words, for the dispossessed. I hoped that he included me even though I was not of the third world but had truly invested.

This dream is about including the disposessed in our spiritual view of life. For the dominant culture of the west, these have been collectively people of color. The dispossessed, the disadvantaged, and the victims of injustice must be included in any attempt to bring psychic balance to either a national or individual level. In fact, not only must they be included, but from the position of the dominant culture they are the way or means by which balance will be achieved. It is here that our compassion will be tested and refined and justice will again become a word with meaning. The dispossessed exist in the world around us and in our own inner depths. If we do not bring them into the "rituals" that promise change or transformation, then it is fair to question our commitment as a nation or as individuals to reclaiming the earth and the Indigenous One who is the symbol of our own dispossession. Forgetting this makes it doubtful if any transformation of any value would be possible.

Yet the dominant culture with its technology need not be the enemy. To naively accept this as both the problem and the answer deepens the split that locks everyone into a victim/perpetrator role. There is enough about this historically that would seem to make this true. Yet the problem seems to be more with the attitude carried by the dominant culture and its use of technology. Technology is not the enemy. How technology fits into our value structures and attitudes, especially toward the land as a whole is the problem. A few years ago I was part of a conference on this issue at a university in Chicago. The night before I was to give my talk, I dreamed that on the way to the campus building where I was to speak, I was to get down and kiss the cement. It was a balancing reminder that the megapolis, with its technology and knowledge, needs to be accepted and, in fact, even redeemed from its own misuse and unnecessary detachment from its natural context, the earth. The dominant culture needs to yield and listen to earth stories and consider earth values. There needs to be not only an exchange of these stories and values, but also the belief that it is possible for this to happen today. Indian people have historically been more open to non-Indian people than the other way around. They have been more open to our stories, more trusting of our treaties, and more receptive to our presence than we of them. Two dream examples show this:

> I visited an Indian man I know and complimented him on the pine wood interior of his house. Then I saw that one room was in fact imitation pine wall paper. Again I saw another room was covered with 4 x 8 sheets of veneer that were coming loose. Yet it did not matter. He decided he was going to have a giveaway for me and brought out a case of jewels that he would disperse to me and others in the evening. I thought I should give him a gift also and decided on a crucifix, since he was Catholic. He was pleased and said the one he had was a cheap $3.00 one. I noticed the cross-beams were loose and needed to be glued better.

Historically Indian people often accepted Christianity and still held to their traditional beliefs. This was not a conflict for many of them. Christianity, however, did not come to the Indian people for the noblest of reasons. It often came with the attempt to civilize and acculturate in the name of Christ. Perhaps this is the reason for the cheap $3.00 crucifix and the not-so-real pine rooms inherited from our own culture. Though the "civilizing" was unreal and inhuman, the gifting goes on. The giveaway is at the heart of Indian "religion." It is based on the idea that all of life is giving of itself, so in turn we also need to give back what has been given to us. It is a stewardship based on an eco-theology, that is, on a recognition that in the universe we are all related. To give this Indian a crucifix, one that is solid and of value, reflects what I believe has always been true, and even more so today, that Indian people are open to the western religious paradigms as long as they do not come with a sword or a treaty attachment. The question is more for those of the non-Indian world: Are we open to being gifted by them both literally with their wisdom and figuratively as reflections of our inner deeper but forgotten selves?

A second dream carries this same theme:

> There was a circle made up mostly of Indians and a few whites. Another man and I came to join them. He asked if he could join them and they said he would have to sit on the outside of the circle. It occurred to me that other whites were there, and it was intended they should be. I felt assured it was okay, almost as though we whites were the reason the Indians had now gathered to talk.

The circle is a symbol of completeness and is central to Indian art and thinking. The circle is the horizon, the bird's nest, the shape of the *tipi.* It is the great Medicine Wheel of life and the unbroken link of all life related together. A subtle twist of the dream is in the kidding, which is a rich form of Indian humor. It is only done to those who are accepted. This is not only my dream but, like others, it reflects a turning point in our times of a coming together as one people and as one circle. The late Oglala holy man and mystic, Black Elk, envisioned and spoke of this early in his life:

> Then I was standing on the highest mountain of them all, and round about beneath me was the whole hoop of the world. And while I stood there I saw more than I can tell and I understood more than I saw, for I was seeing in a sacred manner the shapes of all things in the spirit, and the shape of all shapes as they must live together like one being. And I saw that the sacred hoop of my people was one of many hoops that made one circle, wide as daylight and as starlight, and in the center grew one mighty flowering tree to shelter all the children of one mother and one father. And I saw that it was holy.

The day is coming upon us when the divisions will not be drawn so much between Indian and non-Indian but between those who love the earth and those who have little regard for Her. There is a great sadness in the land today. It is a grief that exists just below the layer of our conscious mind. Just why this is true is supported by the idea that when our home, the earth, suffers, we suffer, and when the Indigenous One is broken, so are we. What we have done to another as a dominant people, we have simultaneously done to ourselves. In that respect, the tragedies of events like Sand Creek and Wounded Knee live in the American psyche as an unhealed wound, since what we have done unto another people, we have done unto ourselves. A great healing is needed today, and a great healing is possible. The earth is as always ready to receive us as is the Indian literally and as a reflection within ourselves if given a chance. It is now time to begin moving away from a blame and guilt relationship into a recognition of our common grief and common brokenness and common task to clean up the mess. It seems it was this that I felt that evening leaving the Faville Prairie not so long ago.

The tenacity of the earth to recover and of the Indigenous One to reach back in our direction is sobering. The closing metaphor for this is an Indian whom I will call

Jimmy. My family and I met him at a Sun Dance in South Dakota several summers ago. Jimmy was obviously crippled, the left side of his body being partially lame. It seems Jimmy and five of his friends had been drinking one night fifteen years prior to our meeting and had been in an auto crash that left him the only survivor. Now with mild brain impairment and a lame body, he hung unto the one thing left to him–his belief in the goodness and presence of Wakan Tanka, the Great Mystery. In and out of alcoholic binges and annual Sun Dances in which he participated, he held to his tradition and belief. The evening the dance ended and after most of the dancers had left, Jimmy invited my family and me to join him in smoking his pipe in one of the now abandoned *tipis*. In the darkness and sacredness of that moment, Jimmy became our high priest as we each took our turn in silence smoking the pipe. When we finished, we drove him to his apartment in a local housing project and helped him carry in some food we thought he could use. Except for a cracked plastic chair and a spring bed with no mattress, his place was empty. This was his home. But what he lacked in material possessions, he possessed in spirit, reminding us through his brokenness about what really is important in life as well as the common ground we all share before the Great Mystery. He became the true image of the Indigenous One, wounded but ready. We left the reservation late that night with a sense of sadness not unlike that which I experienced leaving the Faville Prairie. The sadness seemed bigger than us, and we were not sure our lives would ever be the same again.

Chapter Five

The Indigenous Life: Some Views for Our Times

I am going to venture that the man who sat on the ground in his tepee meditating on life and its meaning, accepting the kinship of all creatures, and acknowledging unity with the universe of things was infusing into his being the true essence of civilization.

Luther Standing Bear (1868–1939)
Oglala Sioux Chief

Up to this point, I have made frequent reference to the word "indigenous." I do not particularly like this word because it conveys a tone of a detached scientific attitude studying an object–in this case, a people or a way of life with whom there is no identity or personal connection. But then the words "primitive" and "aboriginal," which etymologically mean "of the first kind" and "from the beginning," have collectively conveyed inferior, undifferentiated and undeveloped. The deterioration of these words reflects our own loss of connection to our beginnings, and what it means to be "born from within" the earth itself, which brings us back to where we started, for that is what the word "indigenous," broadly speaking, means. I will use this word, then, for the sake of simplicity, to try to convey a perspective of life, an attitude and a lifestyle that, I believe, is fundamental to everyone everywhere. As I write this, I am aware of how inflated this appears, but from a down-to-earth human point of view it is quite elementary. It is with deliberate intention that I stated "down-to-earth human" since that is the perspective that must be maintained in order to proceed.

A simple story will explain better where this chapter is headed. In the summer of 1993, I met a man who had packed his life up in a van and traversed North America looking for what many of us are looking for, a deeper sense of self and soul. Earlier that summer he found himself on a Crow reservation in Montana. It was there that he met an Indian man who befriended him and willingly shared his house and family with him. During their short time together, this Indian friend shared many things, including the deep pain his people had suffered over the centuries at the hands of the American government along with the prejudice that exists to this day. Now this man of whom I speak is a very sensitive and caring person, so he could not help being affected by what he heard. In a pained moment, he said to his Indian companion, "After all that has been done to you by my race, how can you be so kind and giving to me?" His friend grabbed him firmly by one of his arms and replied, "Remember, before you were white, you were human."

To remember that before we were any color, we were/are human is the most simple way of saying we all have an indigenous core. On one hand it is not possible to write a comprehensive definition of what it is to be indigenous because it involves the whole of the evolutionary process. "Born from within" is an active event, an ongoing process that continues to this day as certainly as the evolutionary process continues. The principle of evolution requires that its progressive movement not only anticipates a future but is "born" from that which has gone before. Much has gotten in the way of this process. Much has sidetracked us from remembering where we came from and that before we were anything, we were children of the earth. On the other hand, it is definitely possible to say something about the indigenous life, if ever so overly simple and passionate on my part, though with the greater hope of awakening the imagination to call back what we have left behind. This is not a call to return to a former time and lifestyle but to consider what has been basic to the human race for a good 100,000 years and has only recently on a collective level been put aside. A study of "primitive psychology" is essential in understanding psyche's activities in the fundamental sense. This is not a primitivism in the usual notion but a commonsenseness of human behavior that is archetypally coded into each of us and becomes basic and needful for a healthful relationship to ourselves and the world around us.

ALL MY RELATIVES

If any one thing could be associated with the indigenous perspective of life, it is the keen awareness that one is related to all things in the universe. This is no superficial ecological view but a deep spiritual knowing that all things are related because all come from the Great Mystery and all are endowed with its spirit. To become cut off from this awareness is to become not only an isolated but a truly lonely, disoriented and unrelated/able person. Jung spoke of this modern condition in the last major writing of his life, *Man and His Symbols*:

> As scientific understanding has grown, so our world has become dehumanized. Man feels himself isolated in the cosmos, because he is no longer involved in nature and has lost his emotional "unconscious identity" with natural phenomena. These have slowly lost their symbolic implications. Thunder is no longer the voice of an angry god, nor is lightning his avenging missile. No river contains a spirit, no tree is the life principle of a man, no snake the embodiment of wisdom, no mountain cave the home of a great demon. No voices now speak to man from stones, plants, and animals, nor does he speak to them believing they can hear. His contact with nature has gone, and with it has gone the profound emotional energy that this symbolic connection supplied.[16]

We are always in relationship to that which is around us whether we know it or not. Relationship implies relatives, though these words do not mean much today consciously. But unconsciously these words carry the weight of the world to be recognized as interconnected and belonging to one family. There is a starvation of the soul to be known, seen and held not only by a personal family but by the order of creation itself.

To belong then is to be fully aware that one has relatives, though this goes far beyond one's personal family. Among the Sioux, there is a phrase that is said repeatedly at ceremonies; it is "all my relatives" (*"mitakuye oyasin"*). It is like a creed in that it reflects the individual's belief that the universe is united as one family and that there is an ethical commitment to live responsibly in relationship to all things in the universe. It carries the notion that nothing we do ever stands by itself but has consequences for the broader reality in which we live. It is to know that we are never alone, never an orphan, never cut off. Every ritual is done in the context of "all my relatives" since all my relatives, that is, all creation, are invited into the sacred space and time being honored whether it is a purification lodge, a vision quest, the Sun Dance, smoking the sacred pipe, making relatives (adoption) or honoring the dead. It is the core belief of all that is seen and lived among traditional Sioux people, though not by them alone but by all traditional peoples in one form or another. It is in fact, as already stated, the heart of that which is indigenous to all of us even if forgotten. Everything that follows from this point on and everything that has been stated up till now can be seen in the context of this core belief. "All my relatives" expands the definition of who we are as individuals but also now in the twentieth century stands as a spiritual measure for our sense of alienation.

MY RELATIVES, THE STARS

Science today is continually revealing new insights regarding our vast universe. Not only is the earth given a context within its own Milky Way galaxy that is made up of billions of stars and is millions of light years wide, but this itself is set in the context of other galaxies throughout our universe which is still expanding and still reacting to the Big Bang some twenty billion years ago. Only now do scientists have the technology to see the light caused from this event that happened so long ago. In short, we are able to see the beginnings of time. The idea of "all my relatives" is pushed up into the stars, into the night sky, and demands the imagination to wonder beyond itself. In many ways we are but a micro-moment in a vast cosmic history that in no way diminishes our significance as we might think but rather highlights our importance and raises our dignity in a way that only the stars can do.

Unfortunately, our science has created a broader context for our planet earth than our theology or psychology in the western world has kept up with. Neither discipline has paid much regard to the effects of being cut off from such a dimension of reality as the greater universe provides. Each has been fixated by a limited vision of what it is to be human. Even though we know Galileo was right, we still talk about the "path" of the sun and the stars rather than the orbit of the earth. Similarly, just as Christian theology talks literally of needing to know Jesus of Nazareth in order to be "redeemed," so modern psychology talks of needing to know the ego as the *prima materia* to be equally saved. By dimming the stars, a light has been cast on the human race that has placed us in our minds at the center of the universe. An anthropocentric point of view has set in that has given us an importance far more than we deserve. So it is then that we have little sense of or connection to a cosmic history. It is as though we came here from some place outside the cosmos. Our home does not include the stars and beyond.

I am indebted to a booklet titled *Lakota Star Knowledge* by Ronald Goodman[17] who has wonderfully described the relationship of a specific people and their way of life with how they saw the stars above them. This relationship is based on the idea that what happens in the heavens is replicated on earth and what happens on earth has its parallel in the heavens. Goodman writes, "The stars were called, 'The holy breath of the Great Spirit,' the *woniya* of *Wakan Tanka.* Thus, when the Lakota observed the movement of the sun through their constellations, they were receiving spiritual instruction. Their observations when interpreted by Lakota oral tradition and their star and earth maps told them what to do, where to do it and when."[18] During the first quarter of the year, they watched for the coming of the spring equinox by observing various constellations as they crossed the ecliptic of the sun. These constellations were related to or made up the *Cangleska Wakan* or Sacred Hoop that can be easily seen in the night sky and forms the celestial parallel to the sacred Black Hills with its red formation encircling it. When the first constellation crossed the ecliptic of the sun, the vernal equinox had arrived, and it was time to strike the winter camps and move toward the Black Hills, following, at the same time, the northern migration of the buffalo herds. When the next constellation (the Pleiades) crossed the path of the sun, they moved to an area near Harney Peak. By the time the center of the *Cangleska Wakan* crossed the sun, they had moved to the center of the Black Hills and then finally, with the movement of the last constellation, they arrived at Devil's Tower on the western side of the Black Hills where the annual summer solstice Sun Dance was performed. In short their life and ritual were governed by the stars, which reminded them that all earthly matters have their spiritual parallel as seen in the heavens.

Concerning the sun's position to the constellation and the importance of this to the Sioux people, Goodman wrote:

> In the time-factored Lakota Life Way, to be mirroring on earth what was happening in the spirit world (that is, in the star world) was basic and typical. It was vital in Lakota theology to be doing on earth what the spirits were doing in the spirit world, at the same time, in the same way. The correlation between constellations and earth sites in the Black Hills enabled the People to be also at the right place. The right place was the place which mirrored the stellar position of the sun. The *Lakol Wicho'on,* the Lakota Life Way, summoned the People to do the right action at the right time in the right place.
>
> As we have said, during the spring quadrant, the Lakota were following, mirroring the sun's path on earth. The Lakota call themselves the people of the heart, and to them that's what the sun is. The sun is the physical manifestation of the heart, which is to say, the infinite generosity of *Wakan Tanka.*[19]

In our own time there is little recognition of any connection to the stars or of the vastness of the universe itself having a conscious effect on our human condition. But something is remembered when, uncontaminated by city lights, we look on rare occasions at a starlit night and the vastness and splendor of our Milky Way. It is as though we have not seen it before, though we are lifted up if even for a moment to an awareness of something bigger than ourselves, to a transpersonal dimension the soul has always known. We once had a Zodiac that guided us, but now the "stars" live in Hollywood or on the tabloid screen. I am reminded of the word "disaster" which means "to be separated from the stars" (Latin: *dis,* apart, asunder and *astrum,* star).

This separation has become a psychological truth in our times. We live with what I call an anthropocentric gravity that locks us into ourselves in such a fashion that we can barely fathom a world that does not exist without us. We have so personalized the world that it does not endure in our minds apart from our own existence. We forget that life existed for billions of years before we came on the evolutionary stage. This parochial attitude has forgotten that *psyche* is strong and can endure much if set in the context of the whole that is inclusive of both the transpersonal and personal realms. Many traumas of life, whether experienced in childhood or adulthood, might know deeper and quicker healing if connected to the stars, that is, to the greater context of life. In other words, we try to make the cosmic structure of things fit into our lives and problems so that they become our whole universe rather than trying to find our lives with all its sufferings in the cosmic structure itself. By looking at the stars, psychologically speaking, we are reminded that there is grace in the universe. Life expects healing. I believe, for example, that childhood trauma does not need to be as devastating as it is if there is a loving community of people to hold that child after the violation and convey through this loving containment the universal truth that life wants that child to exist and that the universe can be a safe place. This is not hard; it just needs to be done. It is the indigenous way!

There is a sentimentalization of human beings today that puts far more value on humankind by maintaining life longer than necessary and at all costs and by destroying the environment for personal welfare regardless of the consequences. This sentimentalizing has caused a shadow of brutality against ourselves and the earth by creating an overindulged population at the expense of third world populations and an environmental collapse that is changing the face of the earth as we have known it. Sentimentality is not a true feeling. It is ego's demand to see things only in a certain way and to refuse the suffering that is implicit with life. The end result is a suffering that is greater than necessary and far more brutal in form. This is hard for us in our times. The United States, for example, has sentimentalized itself as the greatest nation on the face of the earth with the best health, educational, governmental, judicial, military and democratic opportunities possible. Today we are made all too aware of the dark side of this vast, overly idealized system. A collapse is necessary if we are ever able to claim our place as a nation of compassion and wisdom. For our original ancestors, life was not cheap but was placed in the context of the cosmic whole. Though life was sacred and held dear by all, it was also cosmically expendable.

THE LAND AS MY RELATIVE

If we have been disconnected from the stars, we have also been spiritually disconnected from the earth as our home but also as a unified living body. Our ancestors knew that the earth was their mother and grandmother and, because of this familial view, held a responsible commitment to it and to all creation that sprang from Her. This understanding created an immanent sense of respect toward the environment because one was in the presence of relatives. Not only were the stars their relatives, but also the tree, the mountain, the deer, the river and that particular cloud above. Everything in the created order was basically a relative to a person, thus placing one in an ethical relationship of showing proper respect to the spirit of any given thing. Matter was living and endowed with spirits manifesting the Great Mystery of all things. Everything was taken seriously and seen as a part of the vast ecosystem. Synchronistic phenomena, those a-causal meaningful connections, were no surprise, for they were implied in an environment that held itself together as one unified system of which human beings were only a part.

Again, sentimentality is the temptation here, a view picked up all too quickly by a portion of the New Age world and others who forget that life also involves giving and taking, eating and being eaten, birthing and dying. At any given place we can reach down to the earth and pick up some dirt and hold in our hands thousands of years of ancestral decay, the remains of millions of creatures large and small that have lived and now returned. There is nothing sentimental about this. "Awesome" or "beautiful" might be a better way of describing it. There is such a tendency to sentimentalize the earth, seeing Her as we want rather than as She is. It is just one more way to keep ourselves distanced and protected from our own earthness.

I believe we are lonesome for the earth–lonesome because we have become more separated from it than we know or our souls can stand. The idea that all things in creation are like relatives to us sounds foreign if not actually embarrassing to be caught saying. But let us fall back on our greatest tool in the western world–science. More and more we are being made aware that everything environmentally has consequences for the planet as a whole. We are aware now of a common origin for all things in the Big Bang theory that stands for the first time in human history as a common creation story for all people. We know through modern physics that all matter, even the densest, is in motion and is hardly conceived as dead. We are not isolates in a dead world, though sadly that may be an adequate description of the spiritual state of much of humankind today. The only way out of this is to open our minds and hearts scientifically and spiritually to reclaim the earth as our home and as a living entity that places everything in relationship to everything else. Doing this, we cannot turn our backs on the consequences of destroying the rain forest any more than we can on the consequences of ignoring the plight of the inner city. To turn our gaze once again toward the earth does not mean to buy a tent and go camping. It might be a way or a help for some people but not for others. It does mean a shift in attitude and values when it comes to placing the human race in the context of an inclusive ecosystem. The tendency is to make this system fit us rather than trying to find our place in it along with the responsible relationship this requires.

The earth is our Grandmother and Mother; She is our mother in the immediacy of Her giving and our grandmother in Her ancientness. Like Her, we are millions of years old in our evolutionary evolvement, though not just us but all of creation. Having this common origin is what makes us relatives. It is an interesting experiment to try addressing a particular tree you know is a couple hundred years older than you by a familial name such as grandfather or grandmother. This can be done quietly under one's breath with no one in the critical world knowing of it. Do this with the same intent as addressing a human relative and see what effect it has. I suspect for most people it would deepen the relationship to that tree, personalize the relationship and create a deeper sense of being gifted if that tree is to be cut down. Here, however, is where the confusion sets in, for either we have no relationship to the tree and randomly cut where we want and how much we want, or we say the tree should never be cut down at all. In other words, we again get caught between brutality and sentimentality. In fact relatives give of themselves and, if need be, even their lives if the need is there. Creation has always "given" of itself for the rest of creation and for the next generation. Humans are not exempt. If we are to take, let us create some semblance of respect and consciousness of what is happening so that dignity and some sense of the sacred can be put back into what has become an otherwise materialistic world. Materialism can exist because there has been a loss of a living relationship to the creative order. On the other hand, just as we need to take, so we must be willing to be taken. This exchange is vital to a truly indigenous view of life and a deeper understanding of stewardship, about which more will be said later.

If there is a loneliness and sadness in the modern technologized human psyche for the loss of a living relationship to the earth, so the earth suffers our loss. No litany of violations to the earth need be repeated here. We have heard them before and in another place will need to hear them again. But much has changed fast and been either damaged or destroyed in the last one hundred years that took millions of years to develop. This is not without consequences. More and more today people are talking about their inner suffering watching the earth near them being uprooted and altered for the sake of industrial or shopping malls or housing developments or expansion of one kind of another that gives little or no regard to disrupting ecosystems, using up good farmland or considering the effects it has on animals and plants let alone human beings. The growing consciousness of these violations has caused a suffering in many people today that is often taken as rooted in one's personal psychology. More accurately it is rooted in a collective psychology that has damaged its indigenous bond to the earth as home. We have made ourselves like orphans on our own planet, with our only business being to survive. Perhaps this growing collective suffering is the voice of the earth Herself and by connecting with it we can contribute to Her healing. Through our suffering, our soul is being reconnected to the land. True suffering has that kind of ability of deepening our consciousness of our relationship to that which has been lost. Our personal journeys must include a love for the earth itself that enables one in even a small measure to feel Her pain.

KINSHIP

It is one thing to speak of the notion of "All My Relatives" in the context of the universe generally and of the earth specifically and quite another to speak of it in the immediacy of one's personal family. Here is where the first impressions of relatives are made. The child's total universe begins in proximity to the warmth of the mother's body along with the emotional care she gives and rapidly expands to the greater family structure. This sets the ground for how that child will view its expanding universe as it grows older. Is it basically a safe or unsafe place? Do I significantly belong to the universe or is my life a mindless waiting for the day of my death? The role of the family is critical in helping to form the attitudes toward such profound existential questions as the child grows and faces a world that indeed is not always safe and fair. But an initial family container that was warm and loving can help the growing child not to identify with the unfairness and traumas that do come with being in life at all.

I fear for families today, first because it seems we have lowered our awareness of how important family life is in meeting the issues just described and, second, because we have a limited concept of what family life is. These two are actually quite related and together present a nearly impossible situation for people today. We have now a codified version of the nuclear family that includes a mother, a father and children. This is the scope of family life that is set as the ideal standard to be established and maintained. We sadly know today how this nucleus has been broken and rearranged in a variety of forms that challenges the family trust levels of even the best of us. Now it is not just two parents raising a child or children but frequently one parent or a blend of several broken families. It is hard for two parents to bring children to adulthood let alone one. The idea and practice of a nuclear family is a cultural invention that puts an unfair emotional weight on all family members and is anything but native to the human psyche. The revival of the nuclear family is only a piece of the total puzzle. What needs to be reclaimed is the place of the extended family.

Indigenous peoples know the place of inclusive family systems. Even individuals not connected by blood ties will sometimes be addressed by familial titles like "uncle," "aunt," "grandmother," "grandfather," etc. Under this model, a family included many people with intricate social and religious obligations and taboos. Many people in an extended family carried responsibility for raising a child. For example, all of mother's sisters were addressed as "mother" and all of father's brothers were addressed as "father." The true uncle was the mother's brother, and the true aunt was the father's sister. The true cousins were the children of father's sisters and mother's brothers. All other children, those of father's brothers and mother's sisters, were viewed as siblings. This alone expanded the notion of family and the amount of support and help a person might receive in caring for one another and for the young.

Added to this is the unique place of grandparents in the lives of children. It is as though they skipped the middle generation and put their energy in helping the children find their place in the world. These are the parents behind the parents and the ones who are closer to the spirit world. These are the carriers of tradition and stories that are meant to be given to children as soon as possible. Several years ago an Indian woman from the northwest told a group of us how her people would periodically gather together to listen to one of the few remaining elder men who could still speak the original language. For hours he would sit and tell their stories. She told us how most of the people there hardly understood him, that children would fall asleep in their parents' arms and how tired everyone would get, but they would sit and listen and try to understand the best they could. She asked, "Do you know why we do that?" Answering her own question she said, "It is because he knows the stories and, if we no longer have stories, we cease to exist as a people." This is one of the central gifts grandparents have to pass on to the new generation.

I wonder about today and what has been lost in this culture's relationship to elders. The older population themselves do not believe they have much to pass on, given the attitudes we have regarding "growing old." Consequently there is a great and damaging rift between children and elders in our world today. This is sad because there is something basic, even archetypal, about this relationship that recognizes that that which is very old has an intimate tie with that which is very new. Perhaps so many older people display what seems to be an undue amount of irritability and what can simply be called crabbiness because there is no one around anymore to hear their stories or, worse yet for them, they have no stories to pass on. Growing old should be a privilege and honor for all people, rather than a cause of shame and feelings of futility. We should all grow old strong in spirit and, if a person has done his or her work, psychologically more integrated. This does not take a college degree or an intensive analysis but a commitment to grow spiritually and struggle with the essential questions that have been a part of the human race from the beginning.

Herein lies one of the essential missing pieces for our children and youth today. They have few or no elders to help fill the gap in their struggle for identity and direction. Without stories from people who have traveled that way before, they are left to find out for themselves. Parents can try, but often they are just too close to be heard or are still struggling with their own stories to hear the uniqueness of their children's with the kind of objectivity and acceptance required. So our children are left with roots severed and the unfolding drama of creating their own stories without a context in which to place them. We know the extremes to which this can go today. Imagine that our western culture were like a person dreaming one night that children and youth were dying in our streets, were rising up in violence and attacking randomly their world around them. This would be an alarming dream with serious issues the dreamer would have to face in his or her waking life. It would be symptomatic for what was going on in that person's life. As a cancer that works in one part of the body really affects the whole system, so the violence in our culture reflects the spiritual breakdown of our culture as a whole. Psychologically the violence done by and to our children and youth is not random at all in the sense that it reflects the breakdown of the infrastructure of a culture that has turned against itself. Such a dream would give rise to a great deal of concern on an individual level. It is no less true on a collective level. The crisis of our children and youth faces us all and rests on the back of our entire culture. Restoring the relationship between children and elders is one very important factor in lightening the load.

Basic to indigenous peoples everywhere is the valued place of the extended family. Recently I have heard that it takes a village to raise a child. I believe this is quite accurate. But another angle on this is that the village will raise a child whether we know it or not. If it is not done consciously, it will be done unconsciously. There is not a parent alive who has not experienced a child coming home with attitudes and ideas that were not taught at home. So the village and the extended family do exist if even in aberrated forms. But I wonder what has happened to the intentional extended family and, along with this, the sense of community-making that few of us are good at anymore. Kinship is archetypal and seems to be applicable to all life forms in one degree or another. In the context of an indigenous understanding of life, there is no such thing as a person without a family.

There are no orphans. One person's illness affects the entire community. The birth or death of any individual is felt by all.

Today, however, it seems we do live in a nation of psychological orphans. I believe there is a hunger today for deep kinship connection on a far broader level than is collectively experienced at this time. I also believe it is possible to think and act on an extended kinship level even in our fast paced society without intruding into other people's lives uninvited. Occasionally we do hear of someone talking of a surrogate mother or father for themselves or their children. Psychologically it is not only possible, it is natural to do so. Just shifting the attitude and view of our world from a place of unrelated entities each going its own way to a system including fellow family members, if even distant ones, might open the door of our imagination that in turn might alter our responses toward a more creative and relational end.

There have been attempts over the past several years at community building based on a notion of extended family. Peoples have clustered together to live communally in one form or another, especially since the 1960s. Some have succeeded; most have failed. Those who did not make it often did not because of broken boundaries. Who was related to whom was often not clear or not respected. An extended family expanded to its maximum in the form of a relational community would, in another locale, be called a band, clan or tribe. It required, as has been stated, rules and guidelines for honoring one another. The place of extended family did not rise with the development of civilization but was part of the evolution of the human species. Its archetypal root still pulls at us and stirs up not only our desire for it but our grief over its loss. The tremendous emotional reacting that is connected to the place of family that everyone has experienced and that sadly is often witnessed in its violent form is testimony to the power and place of kinship in the human psyche. The loss of kinship connections leads toward alienation and violence at worst. At best, it leaves one feeling vaguely sad and unrelated, alone in a world that seems too big to be personal.

Intentional community building that has been successful in our times seems to be so because some understanding of boundaries has been worked out. People do not sleep with other members' partners; this is your space, this is mine, this is ours; here are the tasks that belong to each of us, and here are the ones that belong to all of us, and so forth.

Several years ago my wife and I and three other couples purchased a tract of land for part-time recreational purposes. In our initial negotiations with one another, we not only checked out each other's philosophy of land use, but what our relationship would be to one another. We all agreed that we wanted to bring integrity back to the land in the spirit of Aldo Leopold. At the same time we all had a sense of respect and liking for each other. What started out as just four couples purchasing land together for the sake of financial convenience turned out to be an experiment in community. After several years, the experiment continues though we have learned some valuable insights. One of these is just how ill equipped all of us are in community building. This is not unique to us but is reflective of our times. This is a time of social disintegration coupled with the struggle to reintegrate. Our own personal struggle to define ourselves as community simply reflected the greater cultural arena of today's world.

Our advantage, however, has been threefold in addition to our successful respect of boundaries. First, all of us had done reflective work on ourselves. There was some psychological awareness on the part of the individuals making up this community. It is a fact that if I do not do certain things fundamental to my soul, not only will I not be able to live with myself, but the community will not be able to live with me either. Second, we also all possessed some ability to communicate on an interpersonal level and to work on conflicting matters. Over the years, this raised to consciousness the required tension of knowing what to tolerate in each other and what to creatively and decently confront. It seems this is what is not usually worked out when attempts at community fail. Not everything needs to be or should be talked about, thus making tolerance a requirement in any relationship. At the same time, confronting for the sake of confronting is disastrous and ends in chaos, whereas confronting for the sake of clarifying and understanding builds relationships. Finally, the threesome dimension of our success was the land itself. Our history has shown that when we jammed in our ability to resolve conflict, or got too far afield in our ability to tolerate, our love for the land became the common denominator that soothed sore feelings and brought us back to a sense of extended family and deep friendship. Not all problems in a family or community are solvable or even need to be solved. Often the formula would be, "Well enough of this, let's take a walk" or "Let's go and get that job done," which was often related to some aspect of the land itself. The calming this brought was no accident because the land outside of us is the land within us which we all share, from which we all come and which we all can rightfully call home whether we "own" the land or not.

The evolution of our own small part-time extended family/community has revealed over the years a microscopic cultural map of what the world community itself needs to recover, namely, a place for tolerance of differences, creative and decent confrontation along with the recognition of the earth as the common ground we all share as home and Mother. To suffer the emotional heat of deep interactive struggles, as our little community has done, has within it the potential of reclaiming a good relationship to the land itself.

Deep community is always related to the land in one form or another. Land is a requirement but not land for the acquisition of land itself but land to hold in relationship as one would a parent or grandparent. They cannot be separated without serious consequences. Community always needs a place, a locale, a point of reference to give orientation and help build meaning. Fundamentally, there is no such thing as a spiritually integrated community that is separate from a living vital relationship to the Land. Indigenous peoples have known and continue to know this truth to this day which is at the heart of tribal and land recognition by Native Americans on our continent.

Developing any sense of *communitas* requires seeing the Land in each other's eyes and souls simply because we are all children of the Land. The Land and the cosmic forms of life themselves incarnate us not as entities unto ourselves and separate from the creative order but as reflections back to the greater whole of which the earth in particular becomes the great giver of the dust of which we are made.

Much of the fascination with the indigenous peoples of the world has to do with the longing to be a part of an extended family, band or tribe. Our unconscious sense of this loss and hunger is great in our times. Raising to consciousness our loss of kinship on both its specific and broad levels will certainly increase our awareness of loss and the sadness and loneliness that go with it. It is also the chance to reimagine relationships and explore alternatives to alienation and begin the long journey back to reclaiming extended family and deep community which really means "exchange or serviceable with" (Latin, *com*=with, *munus*=exchange or serviceable). There is an indigenous knowing of these realities in all of us, even if ever so deeply buried beneath the concrete and rubble of our times.

There was also a knowing of this for Jung who early in his career made reference to the difficulty and importance of building good community. In 1897 while still a medical student and newly appointed chairman of a student group known as the Zofingia Club, he stated in his inaugural address: "The Zofingia must form human, not political animals, human beings who laugh and weep, human beings conscious of their minds and wills, human beings who know that they are living among other human beings and that they must put up with each other because they are all condemned to be human."[20]

STEWARDSHIP

The notion of stewardship today has been greatly influenced by religious institutions and a theology based on the tithe. Though most of them speak of "time, talent, and money" as a total stewardship approach, the emphasis almost invariably always falls on financial giving. Certainly most religious communities cannot function well without money, yet, at the same time, there has been something disturbing and limiting about existing approaches to stewardship. This seems so because it really is not just about money, the tithe or even giving as an act in itself. Webster's Ninth New Collegiate Dictionary defines *stewardship* as "the individual's responsibility to manage his life and property with proper regard to the rights of others." A steward is defined as "one who actively directs affairs." So stewardship really has to do with management in relationship to others which can include giving but might also include refraining from giving. The difference is in having a meaningful context in which stewardship functions. To put stewardship in the perspective of "proper regard for the rights of others" takes it out of a knee-jerk reaction as something one is just supposed to do and places it in a context involving others, a context that requires good management and genuine concern. In its deeper sense, it lifts stewardship out of its one-dimensional form of just giving and places it on the continuum of both giving and receiving which is much closer to the heart of what all of life is about. Life is not just about being born; it is also about dying. It is not just about taking; it is also about being taken. As we eat, so we are subject to being eaten. This is the way it has always been and will always be even if we try to devise ways to hide or soften the truth of our own personal waning and loss that comes with being mortal.

Yet stewardship is not about any gruesome truth; it is about an attitude that recognizes the interrelatedness and interdependence of all things and acknowledges one's part in the whole of the life processes. If all in life are relatives to me, then it is my responsibility to manage my part in the total family, which includes gratitude, that is, recognizing what has been given to me, and sacrifice, that is, being willing to let go of that which is mine for the welfare of others. The key always is for the welfare of others, for the common good, for all my relatives. Without this base, gratitude leads to co-dependency and sacrifice to waste. In other words the inability to see what has been given leads to hoarding, which is based on the idea that I am totally on my own and thus I had better be sure I get and keep whatever I can. Equally the inability to say "no" makes a person a target for every charity cause that floods the market today appealing to the guilt and undifferentiated feeling function of the general population. Thus stewardship is about the whole of life and our whole response to it. It is not limited then to the tithe which was not meant originally to limit at all, though now is associated with it. It is rather a total response based on the spiritual understanding that just as life is giving to me in multitudinous ways, so I am to give back to life in the variety of ways I am able. It is really about staying conscious of my personal interplay with life, that I am not alone but am held in a series of vast interconnections to the entire universe. It may be that at some point in my life I am required to give not ten percent but one hundred percent.

Among Native peoples on the North American continent, this worldview formalized in what generally has become known as the "giveaway" or what northwest Pacific coast Indian communities call Potlatch. These ceremonies were meant to convey to the community that just as one has been given to, so now this same person wants to give back. It is a sign of gratitude at its best. Whether it is performed at a birth date, wedding, name giving, funeral, fulfillment of a vow, or other random important events in one's life, it was that person's honor and responsibility to give to the people rather than be given to as is normally thought. It is a celebration ceremony that understands that all of life is performing a dance of giving and taking and that two-leggeds, if they are to live in a balanced way with life at all, must replicate this truth. In fact the debt is against us for what has been and continues to be given in order to sustain us on this planet. It is a reversed ethic from the way things are usually done in the dominant culture that has gotten caught in the shadow side of capitalism, namely, greed manifesting itself in excess accumulation of material items. This is not an attack on material things in themselves. Come to my own home and you will see a great number of material objects. The issue, however, is threefold: Is there a soulful connection to what are in my home? Are they the product of an addictive accumulation of things? How willing am I to let go of these things primarily in my own attitude of knowing that none of us ever in the end is an owner of anything? This does not mean that those who have should give away everything to those who do not. It does mean to be mindful of those who do not have and to stay conscious that the soul is geared to give of itself, a fact that seems coded into the very heart of the evolutionary process that has enabled the human race to emerge at all.

The knowing significance that all of life interacts in a balance of give and take manifests itself in practical ways in our everyday affairs. At the same time, the lack of such perspective reveals an impoverished loss of soul. If we live our lives from the position of taking, we live an imbalanced life. Our worldview will be skewed, our significance limited, and our soul injured.

Take for example the matter of food. It is said that we are not hunters and gatherers anymore, nor can we go back to this on a full-time scale. What we tend to forget in our corner of the world, where every kind of food imaginable is at the tip of our fingers, is that not long ago some of our ancestors still known to us did exactly that, and that was the way it was throughout human history. Has there ever been a time where so many people can be emotionally, spiritually and physically detached from personal involvement with where one's food comes from? The advantage manifesting itself in the abundance and variety of food has paralleled a loss of soulful connection to the food eaten. Most people eat unconsciously because there is little involvement with the food prior to it coming to our kitchen. The primary hunting and gathering done today is at the average food chain market or convenience store. How can it be otherwise in view of our vast population? The sadness lies in the loss of personal connection to the food that eventually makes its way to our table. By this point, we have little involvement with it, if any, outside our kitchen. The meat before us we did not kill, the vegetables and fruit we did not plant, tend or harvest, the bread we did not even bake. It comes prepackaged, sometimes even precooked and ready to be only reheated.

It was not until I realized the loss of my own connection to food in this more fundamental way that saying any form of grace before a meal usually felt flat and contrived, something that "should" be done rather than my soul's personal response to what had given of itself so I might live. So when we think of stewardship as life's "giveaway" in the context of just even the food we eat, we can get an idea of the great imbalance we are set up for and that our soul has to endure, namely, that basically whatever we want to eat is there for our taking. The idea that something has given of itself has been blotted from our consciousness. I believe, however, that our unconscious remembers and the soul that we are suffers this imbalance simply because it is rooted in an ancient evolutionary process upon which the balance was based. Our inner world does not forget these things.

Years ago I was invited by a butcher to go with him to watch him kill and butcher a cow and a pig for a local farmer. I had never lived on a farm, had never seen this done, and had the kind of curiosity that only someone from an urban area would have. I watched as he killed each of the animals specifically chosen by the farmer, cut their throats, gutted their insides, hung them up and quartered them in preparation for aging and packaging. I saw before me the missing event every time I pick up a pound of hamburger or a package of bacon at the local store.

I have thought of this experience many times since then and used it as a metaphor event to take responsibility for what I eat. Though I will usually not be there at the moment of the taking, when we look the animal in the eye or put the seed in the earth or take the fruit from the tree, it must not be forgotten from whence it came. Remembering this as our ancestors did gives eating the chance of becoming a more psychologically balanced event rather than the psychological problem it now is for most of us today.

There is a great deal of confusion in our times about food. Is it the right kind of food? Is it too much or too little? What is good for us, what is not? Is it right to eat meat or a violation of animal rights? All of these and similar questions may be appropriate but seem to miss the main point when set in the context of stewardship as defined as "giveaway" based on the sacred principle of life trying to balance itself through sacred exchanges. Eating or not eating meat, for example, is often defended with a fundamentalist's passion and a lot of sentimentalism. I recently saw a bumper sticker that read, "I love animals–they are good to eat!" This is as detached as someone saying, "I don't eat meat because an animal shouldn't be used this way." Animals are being used this way all the time in the total food chain along with everything else in the universe. Both positions leave out the sacredness of "giveaway" and the kind of respect it is due that only our more indigenous self can know. So if we hunt or refrain from meat, let it be for more meaningful reasons.

But even foods that everyone might agree are "good" for us may not be holistically beneficial if cut off from the "whence" of their being. It becomes food without soul. The paradigms of eating shift if we move from just consumption to imagining it as a "giveaway" for our benefit from other "relatives" who inhabit the earth with us.

Many years ago, my family and I went on a semi-serious backpacking experience that required us to be very conscious of what foods we took with us and how we ate it. We had to walk some distance just to get water, which alone made us very sensitive of every drop we used. One late afternoon, my son and I were near the water's edge when we spotted a dark shadow off a few yards in the rocky shallows of the lake. In a short time the shadow revealed itself as a fine salmon coming within a foot of the rocky shoreline. What I did was not only bizarre but probably illegal. With one bear-like movement of my arm, I scooped the fish up unto the shore and eventually into our frying pan. We still talk about that meal from the moment of the discovery, the waiting, the catch, the killing, the cleaning, the cooking, the celebrating and the giving thanks with a depth normally not felt. It was another metaphor event like eating vegetables from your own garden.

An indigenous understanding of life requires an acceptance that life inhales and exhales our existence not with a detached indifference but with full expectation that the entire individuation of one's being will be a "giveway" to the generations before us and to those that will follow. It is a letting go to a wisdom greater than ours, to an unfolding of human consciousness of which we are only a small part but are required to engage as certainly as a midwife for the birth of a child.

Finally, there is the great "giveaway" to the death process itself. Death was no stranger to our indigenous ancestors. It was a frequent experience that kept the reality of one's mortality ever conscious. Life was dangerous and frequently short. Family and friends often buried their own dead, frequently children or women who died in labor or men from the hunt or battle. Today our culture has veneered over just how close we are to death and the transitoriness of life. But death does not go away, though perhaps it is delayed or hidden from view. Our acceptance of death is part of the indigenous life in all of us whether we are conscious of it or not. Our dreams can casually show the reality of death without ethical implications or concern for personal feelings. This is so because death is part of the total life process and just simply cannot be omitted. To the conscious mind it is not nor should not be a casual event but, at the same time, must be accepted as part of the condition for being alive at all. The pain we feel with loss through death is the same pain our ancestors felt ten, twenty or thirty thousand years ago. What is different today is not the pain but the ability to deny and moralize against death. Death is not the enemy as Christian theology contends; rather it is to die without having lived or to die without having been a steward in the delicate balance between giving and taking that life itself is.

A peculiar and final twist on the idea of life as a "give-away" and the need to be a steward of this process is to extend the notion of giving into the realm of forgiving. Forgiveness is often misunderstood in our times because the raw feelings and wounds that need to be forgiven are too often suppressed, minimized or even denied. "Oh it was nothing," we say. Or, "My religious responsibility is to forgive that person." We either refuse to forgive or sentimentalize forgiveness with nonsense like "forgive and forget." These two are not the same. We cannot forget. The violation was done. What can happen, however, is that the memory can cease to have the power it once had to stop our life; it can wane in significance because in the true act of forgiveness we have permitted life to go on. Forgiveness is difficult, rarely happening in a moment. It usually is a long process which begins with the full awareness of the wrong done and the feelings that accompany it. We cannot go around these things if we ever will move to a place of letting it go, fully knowing it happened but acting as though it did not.

Forgiveness in the best sense is basic to the indigenous mind. It is an ecological principle. Life is forever forgiving its own upheavals and violations. Mount Saint Helens blew a third of its top destroying everything around, yet its landscape is returning with life and an expectancy as though nothing happened. Nature carries the metaphor of forgiveness without sentimentality by its readiness to start again the process of renewal. Without this attribute in the natural world, life would not go on at all.

Though I doubt this has been studied in any depth, it appears that "indigenous" peoples had a strong capacity to forgive the wrongs done to them. It may have cost the penitent some atoning gifts or acts, but forgiveness, that is, making things right again, was desired and expected. In reading Dee Brown's book, *Bury My Heart at Wounded Knee,* I am reminded as in so many pieces of literature dealing with

Native American history of the readiness on the part of Indian people to try negotiating peace again with the U.S. government and their representatives. A classic, typical and, as it turned out to be, unfortunate example was the attempt by the Cheyenne people through their leader Black Kettle to establish peace before and after the Massacre of Sand Creek in 1864. Even though an American flag was flying from one of his lodge poles, one hundred and five Indian women and children and twenty-eight men were dead after a surprise attack.

In the late summer of the next year, Washington decided to make another treaty for peace that resulted in yet another eventual massacre at the Washita River in 1868 in Oklahoma. In this treaty attempt, admittedly being greatly outnumbered, Black Kettle still was able to reply, "Although the troops have struck us, we throw it all behind and are glad to meet you in peace and friendship....We are different nations, but it seems as if we were but one people, whites and all....Again I take you by the hand, and I feel happy. These people that are with us are glad to think that we have peace once more, and can sleep soundly, and that we can live."[21] This attempt at forgiveness and renewal ended with one hundred and three dead Cheyennes, of which only eleven were warriors, along with fifty-three captured women and children.

Should it be any wonder why many Indian people distrust any non-Indian today and often harbor a deep resentment and anger at even the best intentions coming their way by the non-Indian community? This is not the way it was meant to be but rather the result of hundreds of years of betrayal and broken promises. Attempts to forgive and move on were constantly taken advantage of by the dominant culture, leaving the open-hearted to be misused and butchered.

Forgiveness is difficult and at times seems next to impossible. In my own life, I remember once feeling so violated that I consciously chose not to forgive for a full year. The process of forgiveness may require initially and perhaps for some time that kind of position and the anger that goes with it. Yet I simultaneously knew during this period that I eventually would have to arrive at a place where I would consciously say "I forgive it" if my life was to move on at all. Saying it, however, did not automatically make it happen. All I did was open the door of my soul to the process of forgiveness that would eventually lead to releasing me from the grip of the violation. I had no illusions about becoming friends with the violator though I am aware that forgiveness could lead at times to such an outcome. Whether this happens or not, it is vital for the one violated to eventually reach a point of forgiving if individuation is to continue. Forgiveness is indigenous to the soul. It belongs there and is a force in service to the ecology of psychic life.

DIGNITY AND BEAUTY

Just what makes up the indigenous life and attitude is a reflection that has many paths. What has been stated thus far is a meager attempt to describe what seems fundamental to the human soul born from within the context of the earth and the greater cosmic story. It does not seem complete unless some mention is made of the place of Dignity and Beauty. Though not always mentioned in the same breath, they do have a relationship worth mentioning, especially in our times that seem to have little regard for either.

The term "the Noble Savage" has held a psychological grip on many non-Indian peoples throughout North America, especially when the "savage" was no longer a threat to the dominant culture as was true in the eastern part of our country in the early nineteenth century. It is a description that now carries its own insults and limitations of understanding what the original inhabitants were like.

Yet there is a truth in this portrayal that lies in the psychological projection it carried–namely, lost dignity. This is what the white community saw in the face of the Indian, a dignity that they had long ago forgotten. The dignity of which I speak is not that of dignitaries, parliamentarians, kings, queens or noblemen. Rather it is a dignity defined by the earth itself. The earth is the context that births the dignity which knows that its home and place and vision are rooted in the land and the cosmic story behind it. The human being is no insignificant part of the creative order.

Jung experienced an example of this kind of dignity during his trip to the Taos Pueblos in New Mexico in 1925. During this trip he met a chief named Mountain Lake who shared openly his criticism of the white race, stating once to Jung, "The Americans want to stamp out our religion. Why can they not let us alone? What we do, we do not only for ourselves but for the Americans also. Yes, we do it for the whole world. Everyone benefits by it." Asked what he meant, Mountain Lake said the Pueblos were people who lived on the roof of the world close to God, and "...with our religion we daily help our father to go across the sky. We do this not only for ourselves but for the whole world. If we were to cease practicing our religion, in ten years the sun would no longer rise. Then it would be night forever." Regarding this, Jung wrote and realized "...on what the dignity, the tranquil composure of the individual Indian, was founded. It springs from his being a son of the sun; his life is cosmologically meaningful, for he helps the father and preserver of all life in his daily rise and descent." More than thirty years later in his autobiography he wrote, "The decisive question for man is: 'Is he related to something infinite or not?' That is the telling question of his life."[22]

People are ready for but frightened of self-dignity. The non-Indian community has been taught, mostly on religious grounds, that this approximates arrogance and self-conceit.

The human being does not and cannot carry self-dignity because our God (especially the Christian God) is totally responsible for our well-being, worth and salvation. We have nothing to offer our God as the Pueblos do. Even our response to the gift of grace in Christian theology is a gift from God. How can any of us feel good about ourselves when we are so spiritually bankrupt? All shadow falls on the human soul that either absorbs it or projects it on others. Either I am no good or the other person is. If the other person carries the shadow of evil, then it is not dignity I inherit but self-righteousness.

It is a sad condition because there is plenty biblically to substantiate the value of the human soul and one's ability to help one's God as, for example, the text, "Truly I say to you, as you did it to one of the least of these my brethren, you did it to me" (Mt 25:40).[23] Dignity has been shaken from the western soul, leaving a trail of self-degradation and longing.

To think of our own dignity means to rethink our place in the context of our earthly home. The distorted western Christian paradigm does not see the earth in such a manner but as a realm to suffer through to attain the better kingdom beyond. It is a place to which we do not belong, must even deny, for, after all, matter is evil or at best devoid of spirit–and, if such, devoid of Beauty.

Dignity is not possible if we cannot also see Beauty in ourselves and in the world around us. This is not beauty based on a limited aesthetic like a beautiful sunset, a beautiful woman/man or beautiful piece of artwork. Rather this is beauty based in the total life process that speaks of meanings greater than itself, that carries the images of both life and death, of creation's struggles, attainments and losses. It holds the awareness of a wisdom not immediately given to words but to which the soul responds with a deep inner knowing. Beauty is in the moment but reflects a timeless aesthetic.

The indigenous attitude recognizes the beauty in creation, in one another and in oneself. When we look into the face of the "indigenous" person and see dignity and beauty, we are looking into what we fail to see in ourselves. This is the projection we need to take back, the truth that belongs to everyone. Matter can contain beauty because it is the living "stuff" of the unfolding creative cosmic story. For that reason, what we call nature can hold beauty even beyond our ability to understand or accept it. Beauty is hard to fathom as dignity is to maintain. Beauty can be seen in the act of one animal taking another or in a family bonding together at the bedside of a dying loved one or in the warning sound of a rattlesnake. Where beauty is, dignity will follow. What sadness we carry for the lack of knowing our creaturely beauty and creaturely dignity and our rightful place in the total scheme of creation.

A Navajo song says it the best and sets the challenge to rethink who we are:

> Beauty to my left, Beauty to my right,
> Beauty before me, Beauty behind me,
> Beauty above me, Beauty within me,
> Beauty below me, Beauty all around me.

And again:

> Now I walk with Talking God;
> With goodness and beauty in all things around me I go;
> With goodness and beauty I follow immortality.
> Thus being I, I go.

Postscript

It is indeed an honor to have been asked to comment on the writings of this author. In reading the manuscript, I really appreciated it because it provided another tool, another method or means for broadening my understanding of why all peoples everywhere are to be seen as one people. It is difficult to write about or discuss such broad areas as he has done in such an easy to read and uncomplicated manner. I see the writing as a bridge for better understanding the cross-cultural philosophies regarding spirituality. This book is an attempt to help all of us come together–not just as white people or black people or yellow people or Indian people but as Human Beings placed together on this creation we call Grandmother Earth. He helps us understand that each and every human being is a creation who strives for spirituality and for the knowledge of where it comes from and why it is that we have a need for it. This is one time that a book can help us learn from each other to thus be further enhanced and enriched.

It is a beautiful thing to come to a time, a place, a people to embrace what we call spirituality together: when we can work together, not getting in front of each other, not getting behind each other, not getting above each other or underneath each other, but beside each other working and striving as one mind toward the one thing that every human being craves and needs to have–spirituality. Whether it be Christianity, my own traditional way, or by whatever manner we have chosen to express it, the bottom line is harmony–and then peace and happiness. This book helps us to understand that we do not do things to be just doing them. Above all else, the heart of anything we do is to be able to find the essence of spirituality by whatever manner, whatever fashion we choose as human beings.

It is known, believed and said that every good thing comes from God *Tunkashila* our Creator. What better way than through us as human beings to make *Wakan Tanka,* the Creator's handiwork, manifest itself. This happens by coming together, working together and having that kind of understanding that brings about the kind of harmony and peace of which I speak. It reminds me of what my Lakota elders so believed in, particularly my maternal grandmother. She would say, "The Creator God, He made them all. Their hearts are made of flesh and blood." Her philosophy was that in true spirituality there is no such thing as prejudice. The friendliness that we have toward ourselves is the same friendliness we show to the rest of the world and to our environment, whether it be to people, places, things or animals. One need not look back far in history to see the atrocities that have been committed not only against my own people but against people the world over and continue to this day. Yet, we must not dwell on this history but work spiritually together, knowing that one of the fruits of spiritual action is to help bring peace and order to our environment. Only in this way can we make this a better world to live in.

I can appreciate what the author is trying to do. He has not just studied us Indian people with his own personal biased opinions but has taken the time to walk with and through what we believe spirituality is as it has been passed down to us generations ago by our grandfathers and their grandfathers before them. Because spirituality is such a powerful thing to embrace and is so very broad and needs to be worked on each and every day, it is good when we have someone, something, or some place helping us in that direction. The author has given help in these matters. It is for this reason that I say this writing is a bridge for me personally in trying to better understand other people in this world who also strive for what we seek—spirituality. *Haho! Mitakuye oyasin.*

Florentine Blue Thunder
Lakota (Brule) traditionalist, teacher
and Sun Dance leader
June 1995

Notes

[1]*Civilization in Transition,* Vol. 10, Collected Works, trans. R. F. C. Hull, Bollingen Series 20 (New York: Random House, Pantheon Books, 1964), pp. 50–51.

[2] Ibid., pp. 54–55.

[3] Ibid., p. 55.

[4] Ibid., p. 56.

[5] Teilhard de Chardin, *The Phenomenon of Man* (New York and Evanston: Harper and Row, 1955), p. 237.

[6] Ibid., p. 238.

[7] Ibid., p. 255.

[8] Anthony Stevens, *The Two-Million-Year-Old Self* (College Station: Texas A&M University Press, 1993).

[9] Ibid., p. 261.

[10] An excellent account of the political complications and intrigues on both sides that preceded the tragedy at Wounded Knee is written in the book *Moon of Popping Trees* by Rex Alan Smith (Lincoln: University of Nebraska Press, 1975). Also recommended are *Eyewitness at Wounded Knee* by Richard E. Jensen, R. Eli Paul, and John E. Carter (Lincoln: University of Nebraska Press, 1991), and *Bury My Heart at Wounded Knee* by Dee Brown (New York: Bantam Books, 1972).

[11] From *The Sacred Pipe: Preparing for Womanhood,* recorded and edited by Joseph Epes Brown (Norman and London: University of Oklahoma Press, 1953), p. 126.

[12] In his book, *Theology of Culture,* Paul Tillich writes, "[Religion]...does not need to seek for a home. It is at home everywhere, namely, in the depth of all functions of man's

spiritual life. Religion is the dimension of depth in all of them. Religion is the aspect of depth in the totality of the human spirit" (New York: Oxford University Press, 1959), p. 7.

[13] "The Meaning of Psychology for Modern Man," in CW 10: *Civilization in Transition,* 1964/70, paragraph 323.

[14] Ibid., paragraph 322.

[15] "A Psychological Approach to the Dogma of the Trinity, 1942/48," in CW 11, *Psychology and Religion: West and East, 1958/69.*

[16] Carl Jung, *Man and His Symbols* (New York: Doubleday, 1969), p. 95.

[17] Ronald Goodman, *Lakota Star Knowledge* (Rosebud: Sinte Gleska University, 1992).

[18] Ibid., p. 1.

[19] Ibid., p. 49.

[20] *The Zofingia Lecture*–Supplemental Vol. A of Collected Works of C. G. Jung, XX (Princeton, 1983), p. 56.

[21] *Bury My Heart at Wounded Knee,* p. 98.

[22] Barbara Hanna, *Jung: His Life and Work* (New York: G.P. Putnam's Sons, 1976), pp. 160–61.

[23] Matthew Fox in his book, *Original Blessing* (Bear and Co., 1983), has done much to describe how the original Christian paradigm that validated the nobility and worth of the individual in the act of creation was distorted in Christian history about the third century with its legalization and eventual misuse of power.

Index